THEY TASTED BAYOU WATER

Bayou Teche

They Tasted Bayou Water

A Brief History of Iberia Parish

by
Maurine Bergerie

A
FIREBIRD
PRESS
BOOK

Gretna 2000

Manufactured in the United States of America
Published by Pelican Publishing Company, Inc.
1000 Burmaster Street, Gretna, Louisiana 70053

TABLE OF CONTENTS

LIST OF ILLUSTRATIONS

PREFACE

The part of Louisiana which eventually became Iberia Parish has been known to white men since the middle of the eighteenth century at least. Settlement and improvement of this area have been steady, although slow at times.

Not many years after the founding of the first settlements in Louisiana by the French, hardy traders began to come into the bayou country. Bayou Teche was known at an early date. The spelling for this stream has been noted as Thex, Theis, and Tex. The Attakapas District, Fausse Pointe, and Nueva Iberia became known to Europeans, who were being encouraged to settle in this area, and to American colonists.

Natural resources and the character of the inhabitants have contributed to the prosperity and culture of the community. Increased discovery and knowledge of resources have enabled the inhabitants to keep pace with our modern world.

The interest of many persons in the facts and stories concerning Iberia Parish has been the incentive for the writing of this history. Events have been related which should appeal to both the history student and the layman.

Legal documents, and Court House and Church records have been the best sources of material. Histories written during the time of early settlement and old newspapers have added to the accumulated knowledge. Many individuals have contributed information from business and private records or histories.

The destruction of parish and city records by fire and other means has caused a lack of continuity in the history of the parish. This fact has been a keen disappointment.

The help and kindness of the many persons who have contributed to this history are greatly appreciated. This book could not have been written without their encouragement and cooperation.

Spanish Lake
Burke
Navy Base
Parcperdue
Segura
Loreauville
Vida
Lake Dauterive
Lake Fausse Pointe
Lake Peigneur
Jefferson Island
NEW IBERIA
Morbihan
Brousville
Derouen
Duboin
olivier
Bayou Teche
Lacambre
Lee
Loisel
Jeanerette
Lydia
Patoutville
Avery Island
Intracoastal
Weeks Island

VERMILION
BAY

ʃIBERIA
PARISH

MARSH
ISLAND
WILD LIFE REFUGE
and
GAME
RESERVE

Shell Keys
Reservation

CHAPTER I

EARLY HISTORY

What is now Iberia Parish was, in its earliest colonial period under the French and then under the Spaniards, a portion of that section of southwest Louisiana known as the Attakapas District, which District was later divided into the existing parishes of St. Martin, St. Landry, Lafayette, Acadia, Cameron, Vermilion, Iberia, and St. Mary.

The district derived its name from the Attakapas Indians, the region's powerful nation greatly feared by the other Indians.[1] The name Attakapas is a Choctaw Indian word for "man-eater" and was given to these Indians because they reputedly ate their prisoners of war. The Attakapas were in what is the western section of Iberia Parish as well as in the territory to the west of the parish.

The Indians in the eastern part of Iberia and in St. Martin Parish were the Chitimachas. (A few descendants of these Indians now live on the Teche at Charenton in St. Mary Parish.) Those who lived in St. Landry Parish were the Opelousas Indians.

The Attakapas became too domineering for the other redskins; and, at some time during the first half of the eighteenth century, in a battle on the hills about three miles west of St. Martinville, this fierce nation was almost annihilated by its neighbors—the Choctaws, Alabamons, and Opelousas. The land of the Attakapas became the hunting ground for the three confederated tribes.

Although none of the things traditionally associated with Indians—i.e., bows, arrows, pottery or stone axes—have come to light, there is evidence that Indians lived in the Attakapas District at least 1,500 years ago. Pirogues made from logs which

---

[1]Historians have divided the Louisiana Indians into six groups: Caddo, Tunica, Natchez, Attakapa, Chitimacha, and Muskogee. Each group spoke a different language and contained many tribes.

were burned slowly and then scraped bear testimony to this fact. About 1,200 years ago, the Indians began to make pottery, axes, and other crude tools. Houses were built over shallow holes in the ground. A trail from Lake Charles to New Iberia and then along the Teche to Morgan City was widely used.[2]

The first white person to have come within the area of the Attakapas District was probably Simars de Belle Isle. According to his written account of events occurring in August of 1719, while bound for Louisiana, Belle Isle and four friends left their vessel to go ashore at St. Bernard's Bay, Texas, to get drinking water. These men went hunting, delayed their return, and were abandoned by the French vessel. Within a few days Belle Isle was the only survivor.

Belle Isle tells a heartwarming story about his dog. The dog, having escaped when he sensed that he might be used as food by the starving companions of his master, finally returned with a wood-rat as food for his beloved master. One day a panther stealthily approached and was attacked by the dog, which was so badly wounded that the master was forced to end his friend's sufferings.

Belle Isle finally gave himself up to the Attakapas Indians. When he was offered human flesh, which he refused to eat, he was given fish. He was adopted by a widow and made a slave, his task being to carry the bodies of the enemies doomed to be eaten. After a while he was affiliated with the nation and taken to war, at which time he distinguished himself and was made a warrior. Two years passed. Then deputies from a tribe near Natchitoches came to smoke the calumet (a tobacco pipe smoked at conferences usually as a symbol of peace or war) with the cannibals and told of pale faces in the neighboring nation. By these Indians Belle Isle sent, to the white men, a message in a little metal box. The commandant at Natchitoches, Louis Juchereau de St. Denis, sent some Indians to rescue Belle Isle. The rescue party discharged their muskets and ordered Belle Isle to surrender. The savages were terrified at the noise, which they thought to be thunder. Jean Baptiste le Moyne, Sieur de Bienville, governor of Louisiana at the time, rewarded the rescuers;

---

[2]William Darby's *Map of Louisiana (1816-17)*.

and later, when a delegation of Attakapas, with the foster-mother, came to New Orleans, a gift was made to them and an alliance formed. The Indians gradually abandoned cannibalism. In 1776, when Bernardo de Galvez, Colonel of the Louisiana Regiment and later governor, recruited 160 Indians in Louisiana to fight against the English, the Indians did not injure those whom they captured. There is evidence, however, that at times, they reverted to their old ways. In 1804, for example, when a Dominican priest, Father Isabey, was sent to the Poste des Attakapas, he was beset by the Indians, who pulled off the nails of his fingers and toes.

It seems that, during this time under French rule, the government had very little interest in the Attakapas District. The primary reason of the colonist for coming to Louisiana was to acquire riches and return to France to enjoy life. For this reason an area such as the Attakapas remained practically unexplored, with only a few of the adventurous type coming to the outlying region.

By 1723, the French had divided Louisiana into seven districts, with the Attakapas area within the Orleans District. Each district was served by a commandant and a judge for its military and civil needs. The district officers lived in New Orleans; but although there were many navigable streams, these officers seldom visited their territory.

Some time during the first half of the eighteenth century, a few of the more daring French traders went into the Attakapas District to barter with the Indians; and the Indians, in turn, began to go to New Orleans to trade. Before the middle of the century, a few of these Frenchmen settled in the area and occasionally took Indian brides. These first settlers were trappers; but, before long, some of these Frenchmen began raising horned cattle in the prairies.

The settlement, "le Poste des Attakapas," which gradually developed on the Teche, later became known as St. Martinville. In 1756 a priest, stationed at the church in Pointe Coupee, began to minister regularly to the Catholic settlers. In 1765 the St. Martin church parish was organized, land was donated for a church, and soon a chapel was built.

It is recorded that one of the first to settle in the Attakapas area was one Masse, who was of a rich Grenoble family. He brought with him about twenty Negroes, whom he treated more as his children than as slaves. These Negroes scarcely worked enough for their needs.

Masse lived in an open shack, slept on bearskin stretched on boards, and dressed in deer skins. His only utensils were a knife and horn, both of which he carried with him. He lived this way for nearly twenty years, extending hospitality to anyone asking for it; but there were few comforts to induce any travelers to linger there.

One of the first entries in the St. Martin Church records of this time shows that on June 5, 1756, a Negro slave belonging to Masse in the Attakapas was baptized. Many other records of baptisms of the slaves of Masse are available. In 1756 Andre Masse is named "parrain" of a number of slaves. One entry shows that on July 11, 1757, a free Negro, Claudine Leveille, living on Mr. Masse's place, was baptized.

The records of the Superior Council of Louisiana of 1747 offer proof that Sieur Masse was trading in the Attakapas District. In that year, a suit was filed against him by Andre Fabry de la Bruyere, scrivener of the Marine, for failure to complete the dissolution of a partnership according to an agreement made at an earlier time.

Other proof that Masse was in the area at an early date is found in the testimony in the case of U. S. versus D'Hauterive. The records state that Edward Masse and Jean Antoine Bernard D'Hauterive, in partnership, owned and operated a vacherie (cattle range) located east of the Teche in what is now Iberia Parish, and, that later, in 1765, because the Acadians were trespassing their lands, they moved their vacherie to a grant made by the French governor to a large tract beginning on Lake Tasse and extending to Bayou Vermilion. The lands of the former location were given to the Acadians.

On April 1, 1817, Rachel Masse, daughter of Georges Masse and Elizabeth Haisse of Petite Anse, was born. Her paternal grandparents were listed as Andre Masse and Marie Dorothy Howerstock, and her maternal grandparents were Hamelicar Haysse (variation in spelling occurs frequently in records) and Elizabeth Troitt. Andre may have been the son of the settler who had lived in the Attakapas District in 1756. Also, the name Rachel Masse may have been misspelled, or the name Masse may have been later changed to Marche. In the St. Martin Court House records, in a Book of Succession, Andre, Marie, Elizabeth, Rachel, and Maria are named as the children of George Marche and Betsy Hays of Petite Anse. The record states that "Betsy, a widow, is to be married to William Dooley."

The Attakapas District is mentioned in the records of 1757, during the administration of Governor Louis Billouart, Chevalier de Kerlerec. The records show that some Canadians had been allowed to come to Louisiana to settle among their countrymen. Some of the Canadians eventually settled along the Teche. No existing records show just when the Canadians came into the region nor when they came into the part that is Iberia Parish.

On February 28, 1765, Nicholas Foucault, the *commissaire ordonnateur*, wrote to the French minister: "A few days before this 193 Acadians came to Louisiana from Santo Domingo. They were greatly in need of assistance, which was given until they could choose lands in the Opelousas area and become self-sustaining." On May 4, Foucault wrote of the arrival of eight more Acadians and stated that he intended to send them into the Attakapas District. Again, on May 13, Acadian families arrived (this time there were forty-eight). They were sent to the Opelousas and Attakapas areas.

When other Acadians arrived, the colonial treasury was so empty that government help could not be given them. Some private donations were made. Captain Antoine Bernard Dauterive made a contract with some of the Acadian families to give each family, for six consecutive years, one bull and five calves. At the end of six years, Dauterive was to receive the same number of cattle of the same age and kind as given, plus half of any increase in profits. A paper dated April 4, 1765, shows a contract between Dauterive and eight chiefs of the Acadians. These leaders were Joseph (Beausoleil) Broussard, Alexandre Broussard, Joseph Guillebeau, Jean Duga, Olivier Tibaudau, Jean Baptiste Broussard, Pierre Arcenaud, and Victor Broussard. Charles Philippe Aubry, who was acting governor, and other top officials of Louisiana signed this contract. From the above group, three of them—Joseph Guillebeau, Jean Duga, and Pierre Arcenaud—settled on the Acadian Coast on the Mississippi River above the German Coast. Beausoleil was "le capitaine commandant des Acadiens des Atakapas."

In the St. Martin Church records an entry dated 1765 announces the coming of the Acadians. Below the priest's signature is added "cure de la no^{le} (nouvelle) Accadie." The first baptism listed after the arrival of the Acadians is that of Marguerite Ann Thibaudeau, daughter of an Acadian, Olivier Thibaudeau. She was baptized May 11, the day after her birth. The records show that on the sixteenth day of the same month Marguerite Ann died. Marguerite's mother, Magdelene Broussard Thibaudeau, died the following day.

At least by 1760, if not before, it was necessary to obtain the consent of the Governor of the Province to validate land sales made by the Indians. About this time numerous land sales were made by the redskins in the Teche country.

The name "Teche" is said to have come from an Indian legend which tells of a huge snake invading the country of the Attakapas. The savages were struck with terror by the enormous snake, which they thought was too lively and venomous for them to kill. Shooting the snake with arrows, they finally clubbed it to death. The danger of the writhing monster so impressed the natives that the name "Tenche," which means snake, was given to the bayou. Regardless of its origin, a survey map of 1795, found in the Weeks Papers at Louisiana State University, shows the "Riviere Thex," a form of the name "Teche" in use from early history.

When Louisiana was transferred from France to Spain, the government made plans to develop the natural resources of the colony so that the colony could become a source of wealth. The Spanish governor, Alejandro O'Reilly, sent out an expedition, in 1769, from New Orleans through the Attakapas region to the Natchitoches in order to obtain an oath of loyalty from the inhabitants, to take a census, to receive complaints and petitions, and to gather general and specific information concerning the inhabitants and the country. On this expedition the commission spent the night of December 12, 1769, at the home of a Mr.

Flamand.[3] The report to O'Reilly, made by this commission, stated that the lands where the houses were located along the streams had been cleared and that the inhabitants had the advantage of being near the forests as well as water. Since there were prairies between the estates which were excellent for grazing, cows, horses, and sheep could be found there. Rice, corn, and sweet potatoes were raised, not only as sustenance but also to be used for trade with the natives. The report stated that in the Attakapas District at this time there were ninety-seven white men, sixty-nine women, twenty-five male slaves and eight female slaves.

Shortly after Louisiana became a Spanish colony,[4] O'Reilly issued decrees stating that no land grant in the Opelousas, Attakapas, or Natchitoches Districts could exceed one league square. There are no records in existence here which indicate that grants as large as one league square were made at this time in the area surrounding New Iberia. Some grants made contained eighty-four arpents. In cases of necessity a double or rear concession of similar extent was donated. These grants were made according to the means of the family. No grant of forty-two arpents in front and depth was made to anyone who did not own one hundred head of tame horned cattle, several horses, some sheep, and at least two slaves. Within three years the grantee had to clear his land of timber for at least three arpents

---

[3]This Flamand may be the same person or of the family whose name was used in connection with Lake Flamand, the lake now called Spanish Lake. (The *American State Papers* show that Antoine Villatore, one of the Spanish settlers in Attakapas, had his grant on Lake Flamand.) Reference is also to be found of a Luis Flamant whose slave was baptized in the St. Martin's Church at the Poste des Attakapas. This church record is found in a book of events beginning in 1788 and ending in 1801. No particular date for this baptism is given. Also, in the Louisiana Census of 1721 can be found the record of Adrian Flaman, his wife and child. A notarial act of 1770 states that Jean Baptiste Grevemberg is called Flamand. In 1805 we find records which show that before 1800 Barthelemy Flamand and Louis Flamand owned land between Bayou Teche and the Lake Tasse marsh. (By this time Lake Flamand had become more generally known as Lake Tasse—round as a cup.) Barthelemy and Louis, on a map made in the early nineteenth century, are listed for these grants under the name of Grevemberg. Flamand and Grevemberg are names for the same family. The earliest signatures found were written "Grevenberg."

[4]Louisiana was transferred by France to Spain in November, 1762, but the Spanish governor, Don Antonio de Ulloa, did not take over until March, 1766.

from his front line. He had to make the necessary levees and ditches, and keep the forty-foot roads along the levee in good condition. Also, the grantee was to have bridges twelve feet wide over any ditches crossing the road. If these conditions were not kept, the land was to revert to the crown, from whom the grant had originally come.

After O'Reilly's decree that no grant should exceed one league, those who had purchased land from Indians had their holdings reduced to one league square. The excess land then became a part of the Royal Domain.

In 1797, the commandant in St. Martinville was instructed that all colonists who were approved be given two hundred acres and an additional fifty acres for each child. Furthermore, an additional plot of twenty acres was given for each slave owned. It was stated in the contract that, within a year, at least ten acres had to be cultivated.

A Louisiana planter writes of a Mr. Berrard, who, the planter says, was the first permanent settler of Attakapas and who was seventy-eight at the time of the writing. Mr. Berrard's partner, Mr. Sorel, who came to the country with him, about 1764, lived to be eighty years of age. Their longevity was attributed to the favorable climate of the region.

This Mr. Berrard may be the same one or a relative of the one mentioned in an inventory made early in 1773 in which Messrs. Jean Berard and Claude Boutte, residents of Fausse Pointe, were officially commissioned to value and appraise the property of Etienne de Vaugine, whose indigo plantation[5] had been in operation at least as far back as 1764. The request for the inventory was made by Gabriel Fuselier, commander of the district. Witnesses to this request were the owner, Etienne de Vaugine; Paul Augustin Pelletier de la Houssaye, Chevalier of the Royal and Military Order of St. Louis, former Major of the place; Antonio Bernard Dauterive, Captain on half pay; and Louis Grevenberg.[6] The inventory was for the purpose of mak-

---

[5]Indigo, an important export, was a plant from which a blue dye could be obtained.

[6]Louis and Barthelemy Grevenberg registered their brand in 1739 in the Brand Book for the Attakapas and Opelousas Districts.

ing a settlement of the community property of Captain de Vaugine and the heirs of his deceased wife.

The property was located at Fausse Pointe[7] on the Teche and contained forty arpents front by twenty deep on the west bank. The main house apparently was a raised cottage resting on sleepers; it had three rooms and galleries on two sides. There were two storage rooms, or sheds, made of pieux (stakes) driven in the ground. The stakes were covered with straw. These rooms were used for drying the indigo and for other general purposes. A court, or garden, was enclosed with oak stakes. The land and improvements were valued at two hundred piastres (a coin about the equivalent of an American dollar). A separate listing was made of the movable property. A complete outfit of tools in good condition, showing that the plantation was self-sufficient, was listed. Thirty-three slaves were listed —thirteen men, ten women, and ten children. The highest was valued at 240 piastres. Also listed were silver, crystal, good furniture, a hundred pounds of coffee valued at twenty piastres, one hundred pounds of sugar at fifteen piastres, and many ells of cloth of different varieties. Farm animals were included. From Illinois to New Orleans, de Vaugine had debtors who owed him large sums of money. However, he owed a Parisian tailor 120 piastres, a painter in Paris 160 piastres, and others in Europe, America, and islands between. This inventory shows the type of good living and comfort enjoyed, in this period, by some people.

In 1778 about five hundred French people were sent out by Galvez under the command of Don Francisco Bouligny to settle in the district. These were followed by Spaniards. In this first group from Malaga, Spain, are noted the names of Romero, Villatoro, de Aponte, Ortiz, Balderas, Lagos, Segura, and Porras (the persons bearing the last four names were unmarried). On January 14, 1779, a message of Governor Don Bernardo de Galvez mentioned the arrival of these families from Malaga. In another message of the same date, Galvez also announced the arrival of 111 recruits from the Canary Islands, who were

---

[7]Fausse Pointe at that time was the section on both sides of the Teche as it made a bend from Morbihan to Loreauville. Today Fausse Pointe is the area near Lake Fausse Pointe.

to complete his battalion, and of another group of 380, of whom more than half were married.

Galvez said that it would be impossible for these people to be soldiers and laborers at the same time, as the vacant lands which they were to occupy were about thirty leagues from the city. It was thought better to consider them merely as colonists. These 499 men were sent under Bouligny's command to form a settlement on Bayou Teche in the Attakapas country. This settlement was called Nueva Iberia. Bouligny identified the village only as twelve leagues up the Teche and twelve leagues distant from the "churchtown where Monsieur de Clouet lives." (Chevalier Alexandre de Clouet had received a grant where today is Levert Plantation in St. Martin Parish.) In addition to their land grants, some of the immigrant families received rations, cattle, money, and other aids, amounting to three or four thousand dollars.

The Spanish colonists who settled in New Iberia and Terre-aux-Boeufs (now a part of St. Bernard Parish) were not given written concessions but were put in possession of their land by the public surveyor. These families, if they kept their lands, had to obtain, after the Louisiana Purchase, recognition of their land titles from the United States.

In later years some of the children of the original Spanish settlers told that the settlers came up Bayou Teche in large flat boats, propelled by long oars or sweeps. When they arrived at the bend in the bayou which begins near Camelia Street near the upper limits of New Iberia, some of the men went ashore and climbed tall trees. They observed that the country was open prairie and apparently fertile. After landing, these newcomers made camp a short distance from the Teche, where they remained for several days. This area was the original site for Nueva Iberia. Their camp was under a large liveoak tree that stood at the intersection of Darby's Lane and the highway to St. Martinville. (This tree remained in the middle of the highway until the road was hardsurfaced.) At first these people cultivated flax and hemp but, failing, abandoned agriculture and turned to cattle raising, for which the country was well suited.

By 1788 the colony of Iberia numbered 190 people, most of

whom were Spanish, although some were French, who had come under St. Denis and Benard de La Harpe, and others were French-Acadians who had come under Benard de La Harpe.

Among the first Acadians in the area were the Decuirs, Dugas, LeBlancs, Martins, Broussards, Breaux, Derouens, Trahans, Guilbeaux, Bernards, Grangers, Thibaudeaux, Arceneaux, Babins, Princes, Heberts, Landrys, Melancons, and Moutons. Many of these chose to settle on the Teche and soon had comfortable homes. They were described as industrious and honest, economical and orderly in their affairs, and contented with the little they possessed.

Early in the history of Louisiana, the word "Creole" appears in reference to the inhabitants. The word comes from one used by the Spanish "criolla" to designate their pure-blooded offspring. In Louisiana the word Creole meant the pure-blooded white children born in the colony of a mixture of French and Spanish parentage. It soon came to mean the descendants of the old French and Spanish settlers. In the memoir concerning the province of Louisiana, Don Francisco Bouligny states that the Creoles were healthy and robust and well able to take violent exercises. They began to hunt as children and, with no ill effects, could spend the whole day with their feet in water.

Some time after the Louisiana Purchase, Americans began to come to the Attakapas country. Among them were the Smith, Riggs, Wilkins, Peebles, and Marsh families.

In 1785 the districts of Attakapas and Opelousas had a population of 2,408; and in 1801 there were 7,250, of which 3,500 were slaves. In 1810 the population was 13,774.

The Spanish government required the settlers of New Iberia to pay certain public contributions, similar to taxes, non-payment of which would result in forfeiture of their lands. The king of Spain disapproved of the sale of land to the Americans who were coming into Louisiana and in July, 1802, issued a royal decree forbidding the grant or sale of land in Louisiana to any United States citizen.

O'Reilly's proclamation of November 25, 1769, provided that there be a central government in New Orleans for the Louisiana Territory. A regulation of 1795 stipulated that syndics be chosen by the Governor of the Province from a list provided by the commandant of each district. The syndic was a subordinate of the commandant and was to preserve order and general government. He was to suppress public meetings. He was not to allow more than eight persons to meet to discuss public affairs. The syndic was constable; and he served as judge in cases that did not involve more than ten piastres. He was levee inspector and supervisor of construction and repairer of roads.

The commandant had his duties enumerated. He was a judge in cases which did not involve more than fifty piastres. He could veto the acts of his syndics and was obliged to enforce the decrees of the Governor. As military officer he examined passports and allowed no one to settle within his jurisdiction without the consent of the Governor. The populace accepted the government provided by Spain and showed no desire for representative government.

In recognition of the faithful discharge of his duties as *comisario* of Nueva Iberia, Governor Galvez decided, in 1785, to appoint Militia Captain Don Nicolas Forstall to the political and military command of Nueva Iberia and of the district of Attakapas. This appointment was never approved. Prior to 1787 one commandant was named for both the Opelousas and Attakapas Districts, the first commandant being Sieur Jacques Cortableau and the second, Gabriel Fuselier de la Claire, said to be the founder of St. Martinville. The third commandant was Chevalier de Clouet. Later Chevalier de Clouet was placed in charge of only the Attakapas region as its first commandant.

The early colonists usually built their homes with material that was easiest and least expensive to obtain. Most of the country homes and buildings were adobe. Loamy soil was mixed with water to approximately the thickness of brick mortar. On this, green moss was spread and tramped, by men, to the bottom of the mixture. This was repeated until the mixture could absorb no more moss. The adobe was then taken out by layers and used as weather-boarding for house and chimney. Beginning at the sill and going up, the adobe was placed between the studs and held in place by horizontal sticks driven between the studding at every six inches. When this mixture was half dry, it was shaved off; and when well dried, the house was whitewashed. Some homes had no floors or sills. The ground was mortised and round poles placed as studding before the adobe was applied. These homes usually had split boards or thatched roofing.

Usually the furniture had been made by the industrious owners, who thought nothing of spending entire days behind a plow or in the carpenter shop, blacksmith shop, or the mill. The women, too, worked hard, making cloth from cotton and flax, and manufacturing stockings. Many women made all the cloth necessary for the family and the slaves.

Tobacco being one of the exports, rules for selling it and fixing the price were recorded in June, 1777. The planters were even obliged to make reports to their commandants as to the number of arpents to be planted in tobacco. The post of Attakapas was to put all its tobacco in rolls to avoid the cost of shipping it in bundles.

The extent of cultivable land in the early period of colonization was from one to three miles in depth from the banks of the stream. A traveler going along a waterway could see all the plantations of the region. The principal products for the Attakapas District were sugar, indigo, tobacco, cotton, corn, rice, buckwheat, common peltries, and lumber of all sorts.

At intervals on the prairie near a Spanish settlement were little patches or islands of trees. Three of these little forests were called Salvador Islands or New Iberia Islands or, by the Acadians, "Trois Isles." It was here that Spanish authorities gave, to some Spaniards (as a group but not individually) on whose land there were no trees, permission to cut timber. When these lands were sold after the Louisiana Purchase, the Spaniards continued to cut the trees. Because the title to these lands had never been given, the Spaniards were sued and had to pay damages. One of the suits relating to this was tried in 1886. When restitution was sought by the Spaniards, the United States Congress made certain land grants to them.

When Louisiana was retroceded to France in 1803, by the Treaty of San Ildefonso, it was prospering nicely. Many farms were located on the west bank of the Teche. The land on the east bank was used for pasturage, as the annual overflow of the waters made farming impractical. Although crops were important means of making a living, stock raising was still the wealth and business of the Teche country. The population of the Atta-kapas District had increased, and its commerce had acquired a certain importance. Most of the commerce was carried on by barge, but sloops of one hundred tons also ascended the Teche to New Iberia. A visitor to this section could meet cheerful, intelligent working people. He could also find excellent wine. There were few distinctions among the people, and riches did not seem to change the way of men but only added to their comforts.

Stock raising being the most important occupation, the cost of a beef carcass of seven or eight hundred pounds was only four dollars. Game was abundant and cheap; and bread was not much more expensive than in France, as flour was shipped from the West in large quantities. A 180-pound barrel of rice cost four or five dollars, and a barrel of corn, the chief food, sold for forty or fifty cents a barrel. The thing most costly was labor, and that was because of the scarcity of the population.

When the United States took over Louisiana, December 20, 1803, Governor William C. C. Claiborne sent Lieutenant Henry Hopkins to the Attakapas District, as a public official. Louisiana was divided into twelve districts with the Attakapas as one of them. The offices provided for were judge, sheriff, clerk, treasurer, and, at the discretion of the governor, justices of the peace. These officials were not necessarily residents of the community. The county judge and justices of the peace were the only ones who served fixed terms and had jurisdiction only over civil matters. Criminal cases were tried by the Superior Court.

In 1807, nineteen parishes were created and Attakapas was called St. Martin. There were a parish judge and a sheriff. The judge served a term of four years and had civil, criminal, and police jurisdiction. There were annual meetings of a jury of twelve with the parish judge and justices of the peace to discuss and make plans for the administration and policing of the parish and to undertake necessary and useful improvements of roads, navigation, and matters of public interest. In 1811 the parish of St. Mary was formed from a part of St. Martin. The jury and school commissioners were then elected. The parish judge and justices of the peace no longer met with the jury.

DIVISIONS OF THE ORIGINAL ATTAKAPAS OR ST. MARTIN PARISH

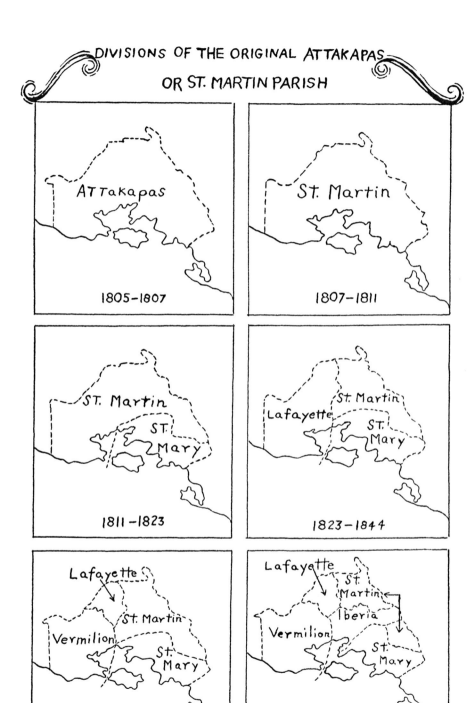

ATTAKAPAS
1805-1807

St. Martin
1807-1811

ST. Martin
ST. Mary
1811-1823

Lafayette
St. Martin
ST. Mary
1823-1844

Lafayette
St. Martin
Vermilion
St. Mary
1844-1868

Lafayette
St. Martin
Iberia
Vermilion
St. Mary
SINCE 1868

In 1823 Lafayette Parish was formed from the western part of St. Martin Parish.

It was the custom for the young people of wealth to go to New Orleans for the Carnival. If they chose to go by boat, the trip could be made in a few days' time. A barge trip, however, required six weeks, as the barge would stop for freight and passengers all along the way at the small portages, which were landing places in the coulees that opened in the prairies of the Teche and connected with the lakes and bayous. The travelers had to provide themselves with everything necessary for their comfort, such as tents, bedding, food, and their cooks and servants. The captain's only responsibility was to see that the passengers arrived safely at their destination.

Because of the small value of the crops being planted and the success of Etienne de Bore in converting cane juice to sugar, in 1795, planters began to try again to produce good crops of sugar cane, which had not been successful formerly. Cane begins to grow in March, and it is cut in October or a little later. It was believed that it was possible to manufacture sugar only in November and part of December, while the weather was still mild. However, it was learned that if the cane were covered with straw, it could be kept from spoiling during a freeze. This procedure assured that all the cane could be ground, and a profit of twenty to twenty-five per cent of the capital invested could be realized.

By 1835 most of the plantations of the Teche had turned to sugar cane as the main crop. In the first few years of 1800 a visitor to this section remarked that the cane grew to the height of fifteen to twenty feet and was so thick that it could be penetrated only with the use of a hatchet. The success of sugar cane on the lower Mississippi caused the planters to be interested in the crop. This change in crop necessarily brought a change in working implements and habits and in the community generally. A number of American planters came to the region and for a while were not usually as successful as the Creoles. Native to the soil, the Creoles were frugal and industrious; besides, they were nearly all stock raisers, which added to their wealth and provisions. Moreover, scattered among the large herds of cattle were the famous Creole horses, another source of wealth. The best and largest of these horses were selected for the horsepowered sugar mills.

After the plantations had been planted in sugar cane, the barshear plow was changed to the improved clipper plow, and the bright steel moldboard was substituted for the Creole breaking-up plow. The all-wood wheel and axletree was replaced by an improved cart and wagon. F. D. Richardson, a planter in the district, claimed that the wheel and axletree could be heard a half-mile away "shrieking like a thousand tom cats having their tails ground off." The *caleche*, which was made entirely of wood and rawhide, was replaced by new carriages and buggies, quite an improvement in style and comfort.

The appearance of the country changed with the coming of sugar plantations. Sugar houses, at first small and cheap buildings, were constructed. Any kind of long low building able to house the four kettles was used. The mill was often outside without cover. Occasionally the old ginhouse was converted into a sugar mill. In 1829 there were only two plantations between New Iberia and Franklin which used steam in the sugar mill. About 1840 noticeable improvements were made in the plantation buildings. The Negro quarters and other buildings were whitewashed and stood in bright contrast to the sugar houses which were constructed of red brick.

In 1853 St. Mary Parish had forty-two Creole planters, and St. Martin had seventy. St. Mary had one hundred thirty-five American planters; St. Martin, twenty-three. St. Mary had one crop of more than one thousand hogsheads of sugar products; St. Martin had none. In St. Mary three planters owned two or more crops or plantations, but in St. Martin no one owned more than one. St. Mary had one community mill, and St. Martin had five; St. Mary had sixty-five steam power mills; St. Martin, fifteen; St. Mary had one hundred fifteen horse mills; St. Martin, seventy-six. The total number of plantations in St. Mary was one hundred seventy-five, and in St. Martin, ninety-three. The average product in hogsheads of 1,125 pounds in St. Mary was two hundred twenty-six; and in St. Martin it was one hundred fifty-five. The estimated average number of working slaves per plantation in St. Mary was thirty-seven; in St. Martin the average number was twenty-six.

Some of the early colonists in Louisiana had Indian slaves. Usually these did not make good servants. By the time sugar plantations were being worked, the slaves were Negroes. Many Frenchmen brought over Negro slaves.

Under the French government and until the time of the emancipation of the slaves, regulations for the treatment of slaves were made by the authorities. The laws, which were fairly well enforced, helped the slaves as well as the master, and regulated the rations, the clothing, the living quarters, and the labor of slaves. Although the food was not varied, it was sufficient and wholesome. On most plantations the diet could be supplemented either from the gardens, which the slaves were allowed to have, or from a garden, orchard, and cattle kept especially to provide an occasional extra supply of food for the group. U. B. Phillips quotes Charles Ball, a Negro, as saying that, in the sugar district, the faces of the darkies shone with all the glint of pork and possum and that their bodies and the condition of their hair showed them to be well-fed.

There were a number of free persons of color in this area. A census of the Attakapas country taken in 1813 showed that there were two hundred ten such persons while there were 1,266 slaves, and 2,270 white people.

In the late 1830's and until a short time before the Civil War, society in this district was divided between the honest and the bandits. The bandits were well-organized, even to the point of having officers with a program of "Robbery." For more than twenty years this group had been stealing animals by one, by the dozen, and occasionally by herds. Honest men deplored the audacity of the bandits but could do nothing even though the bandits were known, for the justice of the early courts had disappeared. Lawyers continued to paint their clients as honest, sweet, patient; and the courts continued to use false witnesses.

As the result of two robberies, one of four hundred dollars and another of one hundred dollars worth of merchandise, a Comité de Vigilance was organized with Major Saint Julien as leader. Gudbeer, the thief, was found in St. Martin Parish and taken to Vermilion, where twenty-two men whipped him two strokes apiece and gave him eight days to leave. Gudbeer had his case tried in St. Martin Parish, where two men were found guilty of abducting him from St. Martin and transporting him to Vermilion Parish unlawfully.

Now that the honest people were organized, it was not long before order was restored in the area.

With the Civil War in 1861 came suffering and trouble; and in April, 1863, General Banks with his Union troops entered the Teche country. Although there was some fighting near New Iberia, there was no fighting in the town, as there were no forces there to defend it.

Because of its location and natural resources, New Iberia was of some importance to the Confederates during the war. Rock salt, which was almost pure, was discovered at Avery Island by a laborer May 4, 1862. General Richard Taylor visited Daniel Avery at the island, and Avery placed the supply of salt at the disposal of the Confederate government. In order to supervise operations and to protect the salt works, two companies of Confederate infantry and a section of artillery, about ninety men, were stationed at Avery Island. Pits were sunk by government agents and about five hundred men worked day and night to take out salt. More than 1,300 bushels of salt were produced per day.

In New Iberia at this time a packing plant was established to cure meat; and Governor Thomas O. Moore set up a little workshop which later became important as an arsenal of construction. Leather was tanned, harnesses made, and wagons built. Cartridges were made by using a large quantity of wall paper found in New Iberia, Franklin, and the surrounding area.

On August 20, 1862, General Richard (Dick) Taylor was put in command of the Confederate soldiers in western Louisiana. When General Taylor arrived in New Iberia he established Camp Pratt. With the cooperation of Governor Moore and a rigid enforcement of the Conscription Act of April 16, 1862, which applied to all men between the ages of eighteen and thirty-five, approximately three thousand men were enrolled. The Yellow Jacket Battalion, under Colonel Valsin Antoine Fournet of St. Martinville, was made up of men from this area and was active in the immediate district and throughout the Teche and La-

The Fight at Corney's Bridge, Bayou Teche, Louisiana and destruction of the Confederate gunboat "Cotton" on January 14, 1863. Harper's Weekly of Feb. 14, 1863.

Fourche country. Other men from the parish joined companies which were active in various campaigns.

Union men tried to take over the salt mine when the Confederate soldiers first took over the salt industry. A gunboat was sent up Bayou Petite Anse; but it never arrived at the island, as it ran aground on the muddy bottom of the stream. The remains could be seen until recently.

As General Nathaniel P. Banks and his men advanced toward New Iberia in April, 1863, Taylor ordered the removal of stores from the village.

After the fall of New Iberia, General Banks left four companies of troops A, E, F, and G of the 52nd regiment Massachusetts with Captain Long in command. He was to keep peace and get for the government as much sugar and cotton as he was able to find. Troops were sent to Petite Anse Island to destroy the salt-works and prevent further transportation of salt. The fall of New Iberia was a blow to the Confederates, as it had furnished them with large quantities of salt beef.

In the western part of town, Company E had charge of about one hundred fifty prisoners, who were kept for a few days in the Episcopal Church before being marched to Franklin and put in charge of the regular troops.

Picket lines were placed on several roads leading out of town. Occasionally the Union men went into the country to secure better rations. They would command the residents to give them what they saw and wanted.

With the arrival of the Union forces, Eugene Olivier, with his wife and child, left his home on the bayou a few miles below New Iberia. When he was able to return, everything within had been appropriated or destroyed. Some of the other places entered and ransacked by the soldiers were the homes of a Mr. Hays on Petite Anse Island, Dasincourt Borel near New Iberia, Cesair DeBlanc on Bayou Petite Anse, and Alexandre Vilmeau in Fausse Pointe.

General Burbridge took possession of the home of John Moore (The Shadows), occupying the lower rooms and flaunting his flag over the entrance. When two young ladies, Elizabeth de Valcourt and Liza Robertson, went to visit Mrs. Moore, they were arrested for failing to salute the Union flag. General

Franklin later took over the residence. Mrs. Moore suffered privations but asked for no relief. Advanced in years, she died while imprisoned in her home.

While in New Iberia, the Federal troops stole the sacred vessels from the Catholic Church and danced in the robes of the priest.

In his history, Alcee Fortier states that the parishes of St. Bernard, Plaquemines, Jefferson, St. John, St. Charles, St. James, Ascension, Assumption, Terrebonne, LaFourche, St. Mary, St. Martin, and Orleans were not to be affected by Lincoln's Emancipation Proclamation.

About the middle of May, 1864, the Federal troops withdrew to New Orleans, taking with them about twelve thousand Negroes. Many of these were forced into the Federal ranks. Louisa Breaux, a former slave who lived to be more than one hundred eighteen years old, said that her father was one of those who was forced to join the Union ranks when the occupation ended. He was never seen again by his family. Louisa was the slave of a Breaux family who lived near Lake Fausse Pointe. When the Union men came, the Breaux tried to hide the silver and valuables. For a few years after obtaining freedom, Louisa stayed with her master or, to use the familiar French term, her "parent"; then she ran away to marry.

Economically and politically the South suffered, and so did the Teche country. Normal progress was held back by the problems of Reconstruction. According to J. D. B. DeBow, about one-fourth of the Negro laborers died or were disabled during the first five years of freedom. It was during this period of Reconstruction that Iberia Parish was formed.

On March 15, 1848, G. W. Scranton, a senator in the Louisiana State Legislature, offered a resolution requesting that a new parish, Iberia, be formed from parts of St. Martin and St. Mary parishes. Two years after, on March 21, 1850, the State Legislature instructed the State Engineer to ascertain, from surveys made by United States surveyors or otherwise, the territory or land which would be contained in the proposed Iberia Parish, and to indicate the area which would be contained therein as well as the area which would remain in each of the parishes of

St. Martin[8] and St. Mary. This information was to be set forth in a report together with a map and any other information relative to the subject which would enable the General Assembly to decide at the next regular session whether or not a new parish could be created in conformity to Article Eight of the Constitution. The assessors of St. Mary and St. Martin parishes were requested to make correct lists of the voters in their respective parishes who would be residing within the limits of the proposed parish of Iberia. This information also was to be ready for the next regular session of the General Assembly.

This work for the new parish was not completed at the time and was further delayed by the war. Again preliminary work was done, much of it in the home area by Joachim Etie, and in New Orleans by Alfred Duperier. Senator Ray presented the bill for the formation of the parish; and the Legislature, on October 30, 1868, approved the act which established the parish of Iberia.

The first officers of the parish were: Sheriff, James Criswell; Parish Recorder, Patrick E. Burke; Clerk of Court, P. L. Renoudet; District Attorney, James L. Belden; and Parish Judge, E. J. Etie.

The parish was divided into four wards. In the first existing minutes of the Police Jury of August 2, 1870, D. Ker is listed as president, and A. Segura, U. Decuir, T. Viator, A. Gibson, N. Miguez, B. D. Dauterive, and C. Provost as representatives of the wards.

---

[8]In the New Iberia *Enterprise*, March, 1889, F. D. Richardson wrote that "old St. Marie and St. Maur (as Evangeline has it) were immovable" in their opinion of wanting to keep their parishes as they were.

CHAPTER II

EARLY SETTLERS AND HOMES

Many families in Iberia Parish can find records of their ancestors as far back as the eighteenth century. Such names as Masse, Thibaudeau, Broussard, Suret, Poirier, Landry, Duga, LaBauve, Dauterive, Trahan, Hebert, LeBlanc, Bergeron, Boudreaux, Babinaux, Carlin, de la Houssaye, de Vaugine, Flamand, Degruis, Berwick, Berard, Coleta, Derouan, Agilar, Dominges, Etier, Fuselier, Gonsoulin, Grevenberg, Henderson, Lopez, Sorrel, Migues, Romero, Gatt, Martin, Fagot, Segura, DeBlanc, Olivier de Vezin, Boutte, and Borel are to be found in church and court house records of St. Martin and Iberia Parishes preceding 1800.

According to the names and dates, it seems conclusive that the French were the first to settle in what is Iberia Parish. Some French settlers were here by the middle of the eighteenth century. Then, starting in 1765, Acadians began to come. The Spaniards came and were the first to settle and form a colony where New Iberia is located. Then came some Americans in the early nineteenth century and next, the Germans. Of course, mingled with the eighteenth century settlers were others not mentioned as a group, as there were a few Germans, Americans, and scatterings of other nationalities here at the beginning of the 1800's.

It is believed that Frank Del Buono was the earliest Italian immigrant to come to New Iberia. Other Italian names recorded in the last quarter of the nineteenth century are Cordova, Jennaro, Briganti, Culotta, Pecoraro, and Drago.

Another group that came to Iberia Parish is the Syrian. The Syrians began coming in the late 1880's. The first names noted in records are Dominique and Soloman. Among others who came a little later were the Jones (Haddad), Ashy, Ackel, Doumit, Elias, Sliman, and Betar families.

In documents of 1727-1730, found in the Louisiana Historical Quarterly, the name of Captain Renaut D'Hauterive is men-

An Acadian Homestead in Louisiana. Sketched by A. R. Waud for Harper's Weekly, December 8, 1866. (From the collection of Leonard V. Huber)

tioned. On two occasions, in legal papers dated 1734, Sieur D'Hauterive, Captain of a Marine Company in New Orleans, is referred to. Whether this is the same family as Jean Antoine Dauterive is not known. It is known, however, that Jean Antoine Bernard Dauterive owned land in the Attakapas District at an early date and was active in the affairs of the area. It is said that it was he who donated the land on which was built the first Catholic Church in Poste des Attakapas.

One of the interesting and lovely homes located about three miles from New Iberia and a few hundred yards from Bayou Teche was Belmont. It was built, about 1765, for a Spanish official who was in charge of this particular section. Fuselier de la Claire was the commandant of the postes of Opelousas and Attakapas at this time; and, although the fact that he owned land around St. Martinville and approximately where Breaux Bridge is located is known, it is not a certainty that he was the official who owned Belmont.

Belmont was, at first, a two-story raised cottage; but in time the first story was removed, and the upper story became the first. The walls were of adobe and unburned brick made of clay and straw dried in the sun.

When, in 1855, Mary Peebles of Hopkinsville, Kentucky, married John Fletcher Wyche, her parents gave her one of their many estates, which, in this case, was Belmont Plantation.

During the Civil War, Banks and his company of Cavalry officers occupied Belmont for several months. While there, the men removed the keyboard and strings of a rosewood piano and put the case in the yard to be used as a trough to water their horses. When the family returned, the piano case was made into a table.

With the passing of time, many precious furnishings, much silver, china, glassware, portraits, and some art objects became a part of the "home" of the Wyche family. All of these heirlooms, together with the house, were completely destroyed by fire in the early morning hours of May 30, 1947. Today another home built in the same style replaces the original.

An interesting sidelight of the Wyche family concerns one of the slaves who accompanied his master to war. The slave, Harry Mahoney, had been taught to read and write by Mrs. Wyche, and during the carpetbag regime he was elected to the Louisiana Legislature. He was the last Negro expelled from the Legislature.

Paul Augustin Le Pelletier de la Housaye was one of the early settlers whose document of title for a grant in the Attakapas was dated September 18, 1771. He owned large tracts of land around the area of Morbihan. De la Houssaye was the brother-in-law of Etienne de Vaugine.

Among people in the Spanish Colony of Nueva Iberia who received help in the form of loans of money, tools, animals, and other necessary things, are some names not of Spanish origin. Among those to whom the Spanish government gave help at the time of settlement and for several years after were Gonzalo de Prado, Don Juan Migues, Francisco Ortiz, Juan Lopez, Miguel Romero, Josef Artacho, Juan Garido, Antonio Viilatoro, Raphael Vidal, Gavriel Lopez, Francisco Segura, Julian Aguilar, Bernardo Aponte, Francisco Banderas, Dona Maria Cabrera, Don Pedro Harpin de la Gautrais, Josef Fernandes, Josef Poras, and Don Luis Pellerin.

Don Nicolas Forstall was in charge of the colony. In his absence Don Tomas de Aragon took charge. In the document relating to the settlement, appear the names of Aragon and Loisel, both of whom signed as witnesses to signatures. Thomas Berviquet (Berwick) was named as surveyor of the district without wages from the king. Perhaps this was because he also received help. Also mentioned are Boutte, who built houses, Colette, and Saint Marc (Darby).

Another of the early grantees under the Spanish government was Jean Baptiste St. Marc D'Arby. The original D'Arby immigrant to Louisiana was Jonathan D'Arby, an Englishman, who sailed for Louisiana from La Pallice, France, in 1719, and was married in New Orleans in 1737. The D'Arby family lands were east, southeast of Spanish Lake. St. Martin records prove that the family was here in 1777 if not before.

In 1813, a beautiful home was built for Francois St. Marc Darby.[1] In 1845 the home was acquired by Louis St. Marc Darby and, in 1897 it was owned by Octave Darby. The structure, of Louisiana colonial style, was built on a hill facing Spanish Lake on the road now called Darby Lane. At present it is greatly deteriorated. It is a two-story building with the lower floor constructed of brick and the upper of cypress boards. The lower floor is level with the ground, and on the right, in front, steps lead to the upper gallery. The round stuccoed brick columns go up the height of both stories. When the place was built, and

---

[1]Many of the signatures for this family found on early documents are signed "D'Arby de St. Marc."

for years after, it was an impressive home. This Darby place has been referred to in some writings as St. Maur's plantation.

Although the Darby family was prosperous, keeping a home in Paris and in New Orleans, as well as in the Attakapas District, unfortunate circumstances later brought a change in the manner of living. Friendliness and hospitality were shown to all, and many lavish entertainments were held in their country home.

Louis Charles de Blanc de Neuveville, another early settler, was the son of Marie des Douleurs Juchereau de Saint Denys and Cesar de Blanc who, at the time of Louis Charles' birth, was the commandant of Fort St. Jean Baptiste in Natchitoches. Records show that the twelfth child of Louis Charles de Blanc was born in Natchitoches in October 1794. Louis de Blanc was the last commandant of the Attakapas Post from 1796 to 1803. Records indicate that he owned a large tract of land in the general area of what may be said to be northwest and west of New Iberia at the time of the Louisiana Purchase.

The de Blanc grant came to within a hundred feet of the present French Street. The southern portion of this grant was sold to Francois Darby; then it passed to St. Marc Darby and to Dr. Leonard J. Smith, whose first wife was a Darby.

Dr. Smith came to New Iberia from London by way of Maryland and Opelousas. About 1838, on the bayou bank, Dr. Smith built a two-story home, which still stands today. Along the edge of the gallery there are columns which give it the appearance of a plantation home. When Dr. Smith's son, Leopold, was born, the father commemorated the event by planting two oak trees in front of his home. Mrs. Marie Celeste Darby Dubuclet later owned and occupied the home until December, 1866, when the house was sold to Dr. Hilliard.

In 1867, after the death of Dr. Robert C. Hilliard, caused by yellow fever, his widow kept a hotel in this house. When he was here on his first visit, the great actor, Joe Jefferson, was one of the guests at this hotel. Among some of the many owners of this home, or hotel, were Mrs. William Jackson, Mrs. W. A. Hatch, and the Webb family. The place, at different times, was called Live Oak Hotel; Alma House, when kept by C. P. Smith;

the Elks Apartment House under the ownership of Dr. Loy Olivier.

Some of the de Blanc land that Dr. Smith eventually possessed became, after many sales, the property of Harvey Hopkins. In 1854, Hopkins made the lower part of his plantation the Hopkins Addition to New Iberia, which began at the northern limits of town and extended to Corinne Street. Harvey Hopkins, about 1853, gave land for the Episcopal Church and for the Protestant cemetery, Rose Hill. After the death of Hopkins, more of the plantation was subdivided by his widow.

Dr. Stubinger, a native of Maryland, practiced here from the early 1830's until about 1878. About 1851 he built, on the south side of Main Street, a home which was separated from the Episcopal Church by Jefferson Street.

John Stine acquired land south of and adjoining the de Blanc land. His land fronted the Teche and went to about what is Iberia Street. This land had been first settled upon, claimed, and cultivated by Francois Prevost during Spanish rule.[2] In 1795 or a little earlier, John Stine claimed, by cultivation and residence, part of Grand Cote, now called Weeks Island. This he ceded, not long after, to William Weeks, who held part of the island. John Stine came here from Pennsylvania. His daughter married Josiah French, who came from New York, hence the name French Street. The Stine residence stood slightly back of the old Courthouse, now the Colonial Theater. This house was torn down about 1884, and much of the home site was bought by de Valcourt and Taylor and later by de Valcourt. In 1861,

---

[2]Louis Segura, a son of one of the original Spanish colonists, built a home on the corner of Main and Swain Streets. This house was for a long time known as the Max Mattes home. Segura moved away from the residence and the place was unoccupied for some time. It was thought by some people that the house was inhabited by ghosts. Some of the later owners of this house were Pat Heirs, William Kramer who set up a bakery and a confectionary in the building, Charles Flockerize, and Max Mattes. Later when the property was acquired by John R. Taylor the old home was dismantled, in 1927, to make way for the Gulf Tire Station. Other tradition handed down says that in 1775, on this land at the corner of Main and Swain Streets, a home was erected by the Spanish government for a Spanish officer. The timbers of the house were mortised and put together with wooden pins. Brick and mortar filled the walls. Heavy brick work was used in the basement which had around the walls "rings" used to confine slaves and prisoners.

the town bought, as a site for the town market, the lot where the City Hall stands.

Dr. Schreiner lived in the second house from the corner of Main and French Streets on the south side. It is interesting to note that at his second marriage Dr. Schreiner was angered at having a "charivari."[3] The din of the serenaders continued for several nights; finally the crowd was invited in for refreshments.

In the 1870's the next house down was Dayton House, a hotel belonging to Dayton de Valcourt.

Next to Dayton House was the lot bought from Dr. L. J. Smith by Augustin Bergerie, whose home was located there. The People's National Bank is on a part of this property.

On the corner of Main and Iberia, or Petite Anse Street, was property owned in the 1850's by Mrs. Leontine Miguez, wife of Jean Fontelieu. Jean's son, Theodore, becoming embittered, forsook the Democratic Party in 1872 and joined the Republican Party. He furnished the white element and the brain which enabled the Republican party to control the parish for several years. He was elected Parish Judge in 1872, then District Judge. In 1884, he was defeated by Fred L. Gates.

The next grants which were held at the time of the Louisiana Purchase were those belonging to Francois Collet, Joseph Carline, and Edward C. Nicholls. The Carline tract was claimed, during the Spanish regime, by settlement and cultivation and was sold to Philippe Boutte after Louisiana became United States territory. In 1810 it became the property of Edward Church Nicholls, a Virginian and friend of Thomas Jefferson and the grandfather of one of Louisiana's governors. The property was later bought by John F. Miller and then inherited by his niece, Mrs. John Lloyd Lewis.

John B. McCarty owned the tract of land next to that of Nicholls. His heirs sold it, in 1810, to Daniel Clark. This was

---

[3]In this section when a widower married a woman younger than himself who had not been previously married, the friends and neighbors came with musical instruments, pans, bells, horns, and other noise-makers to serenade the couple with as much noise as possible. The merry-makers did not cease making the discordant sounds until they were invited in for refreshments. The tradition was that the serenading group could return night after night for twenty times if they were not invited in by the couple.

twenty arpents along the Teche, extending to about one hundred feet above Ann Street. This McCarty land was involved in the famous Myra Clark Gaines litigation, one of the most celebrated private litigations in the history of the United States. Executors, under the will of Daniel Clark, sold the whole McCarty tract, and it passed into the ownership of John F. Miller and his mother, Mrs. Sarah Canby. Twenty-five years after Clark's death, Myra, finding that she was his daughter, claimed to be his universal legatee under a will made by him at a later date to that probated, and under which the estate property had been sold. In 1836 or 1837, claiming that a will in her favor had been made and utterly destroyed, Myra began litigation for recovery of extensive and valuable tracts of land, including that tract sold to John F. Miller. Evidence was produced which convinced the courts, and Myra obtained judgments recognizing her rights. Probably because of this litigation and the cloud on the title, practically no permanent improvements were placed on the Mc-Carty tract, except a one-story wooden residence, which may even have been erected prior to questioning. This home was occupied, from 1856 to about 1870, by James A. Lee. John F. Miller built a plantation home, sugar-house and other buildings on a tract of land above the McCarty property. In 1869 litigation was brought, by Myra Clark Gaines, against Mrs. Cordelia D. Lewis, John Miller's niece. A compromise was made, and the title of this tract made to Mrs. Lewis. The property was then surveyed and streets were opened: Peebles Avenue, Lewis Avenue, Lee Street, and Ann Street. The Lewis land was sold in lots during the 1880's and 1890's. Some of the purchasers were Paul Suberbielle, Walter Burke, Grayson Morrell, Miss Nannie Peebles, and M. W. Fisher.

According to maps made at the time of the Louisiana Purchase, the next land grant going toward the east was that of Francois C. Boutte. This was a large grant; and, like many others, it was on both sides of the bayou.

Tradition has it that Boutte was one of two brothers from France who owned much property around New Orleans and that, when he refused to salute O'Reilly, the new governor for Spain, he was thrown into jail.

Francois' brother, Antoine, whose sojourn in the Attakapas

area preceded that of his brother, asked for land on the Teche in the Attakapas; and a patent for this, dated March 20, 1779, was signed by Galvez. In 1808, this land was sold to David Smith.

Judge Gates bought the property and built a home where the Gebert Live Oak is. This oak, planted in 1831 above the grave of a child of the Marsh family, was an eight year old tree at the time of planting.

John Emmer owned the property where, at a later date, George Labau had his home. The Labau home now belongs to the James P. Cross family.

The Joseph Carline land in the Henshaw addition was sold to Francois Maingonnat who, it is believed, had dealings with Jean Laffite. In 1813, Francois Maingonnat sold his property to Elizabeth Norwood, a free woman of color. In 1828, a deed was passed in New Orleans by which the property was sold to John C. Marsh, who came here from New Jersey. In the 1850's Marsh gave this property to his son-in-law, A. B. Henshaw, who was the grandfather of the author, Nevil Henshaw. (Nevil Henshaw wrote several novels about this section of Louisiana.)

Elizabeth Norwood was the only free person of color, prior to the Civil War, who owned waterfront land in New Iberia. By 1781, other Negroes, however, had received Spanish grants for land along Bayou Teche in the Attakapas District. Free colored people also had slaves, and in 1858 the free colored numbered one to ten as compared to slaves.

Jonas Marsh, John's brother, owned Marshfield, a large holding, east of the Teche, about three miles from New Iberia. Descendants of Jonas Marsh include the families of Cade, Smedes, King, and de Valcourt. Captain C. T. Cade was sheriff of the parish and, for many years, was the most powerful political leader in this section of the state. During the 1890's he organized and largely controlled the "Regulators."

Next above the Henshaw place was the David Weeks estate, which was bought in September, 1825. It measured four and a half arpents along the bayou with a depth of forty arpents. David Weeks also bought an arpent of land fronting the east side of the bayou, with a depth of ten arpents and lying opposite the tract on the west bank of the bayou. This was bought, with

The Francois St. Marc Darby House—1813

"The Shadows," the home of the late Weeks Hall, built by the Weeks family in 1830. Now the property of National Trust for Historic Preservation of Washington, D. C.

all improvements, for $1,567.00. The brick foundation of the home west of the bayou, which still remains underground, was thought to contain treasure; but many have been disappointed in their search for this legendary wealth. At present the home of Dr. H. J. Dauterive is located there.

In 1830, David Weeks had his slaves build, on the bayou, a home that was given the name "The Shadows." The oblong house is of rich pinkish brick; it has eight masonry Doric columns, which rise to the height of the two stories. There are three attic dormer windows on the south front. There is a paved cellar, which is possible because the ground line of the house is twenty feet above the bayou. The first floor is level with the ground. The outside staircase is a typical Louisiana architectural feature. There is a second stairway inside. The lower and upper stories are identical, containing three rooms across and two rooms deep. In the formal garden is a sundial dated 1827.

For a while in the twentieth century the house was unoccupied except for a caretaker; then Weeks Hall restored it to its original condition. It is now in the care of the National Trust for Historic Preservation, to be preserved in its present condition as a house and garden museum.

Some of the Germans who came here to establish homes in the nineteenth century were the Lutzenbergers, the Simons, the Koches, t h e Brunners, Hausers, Schutzmanns, Leitmeyers, Fasnachts, Indests, Emmers, Baumans, and the Fishers. The Lutzenbergers established a foundry; the Fishers furnished the community with a mayor.

The Olivier family that settled about four miles east of New Iberia some time before the Civil War were descendants of Pierre Francois Marie Olivier de Vezin, who was born in Nancy, France, settled at St. Maurice in Canada, and then came to New Orleans. In 1898, Pierre Francois' grandson was married in St. Martinville. Three of his sons, Alexandre, Eugene, and Robert, owned the Olivier Plantation in Iberia Parish. In its day the Olivier home was famed for its elegance, hospitality, and good living.

On the Teche at Jeanerette is Bayside, built in 1850 by Francis Richardson, a friend and classmate of Edgar Allan Poe. The house is of brick and has six Doric columns. During the Civil

War when the Federal soldiers were approaching, Richardson had the bridge leading to his home piled high with hay and set afire. This protected his home, but did not ignite the enemy's gunboats as Richardson had hoped.

Dulcito, surrounded by oak, magnolia, and pecan trees, was the home built about 1788 by Dauterive Dubuclet on a Spanish land grant overlooking Spanish Lake. It is a house raised on high pillars with a wide gallery on three sides. The original walls were of adobe, and heavy cypress was used for the frame. The enclosed staircase, as well as all parts of the house, was constructed without the use of nails. The customary wooden pegs were used in putting together all parts of the house. Some of the original hand blown panes are still in use in the home. In recent years it has come into the possession of B. F. Trappey's Sons, Incorporated, from the Pharr family and many of the original characteristics of the home have been restored.

The families mentioned are only a few of the many that settled here. Many records of the early grants have been lost; many grants were made and not recorded; and some lands thought to be abandoned were granted to new arrivals after they had already been given to others. Family histories reveal these facts.

CHAPTER III

AGRICULTURE AND AGRICULTURAL PRODUCTS

Of the 820 square miles in Iberia Parish 235 square miles (more than one-fourth) are lakes, bays, bayous, and streams. There are also extensive marshes. Generally the elevations range from about thirty-five feet above sea level in the northern part of the parish to barely above sea level in the coastal marshes. The highest land, which is at Avery Island, is approximately 154 feet above the surrounding marshes. New Iberia is about eighteen feet above sea level.

Like any other place, at times this section has had unusual weather. In April, 1885, a cyclone forced Leopold DeBlanc, of Petite Anse, from his harrow and hurled him eighteen feet into the air. The victim suffered head and leg injuries and was senseless for a half hour.

Snow began to fall February 15, 1895, and then the worse "snowstorm" remembered in the area occurred. About fifteen inches of snow fell, and drifts were often twice that depth. The temperature fell to about fifteen degrees.

During this harsh weather the engine house of Steam Fire Company No. 1 was opened to tramps, who called themselves Mulligan's Brigade and named the place the "St. Charles Hotel." About twenty-five vagrants stayed there, and for breakfast one morning there were thirty.

For a year from the middle of June, 1898, the weather was extraordinary in a variety of ways. The heat was so intense and incessant in June, 1898, that a man working in the garden of the Catholic parsonage was stricken and died a few hours later. At least two horses died from the heat. In February, 1899, because of snow and extreme cold, schools were closed for about a week. The temperature fell to about seven degrees. On March 29, 1899, a week after the spring equinox, the temperature dropped to thirty-six degrees. A rainfall of more than four inches fell in one and a half hours on June 5, 1899.

Most unusual also was the flood of 1927 which was a great disaster to Iberia Parish destroying crops for many farmers and harming prosperity generally. It was the greatest flood ever known in this part of the country and was caused by the vast amount of water draining into the Mississippi and Atchafalaya Rivers when the ice and heavy snows of the severe winter melted and by the heavy rains which came at the same time.

Many people did not believe that the flood would be bad enough to force them to leave home. Some remembered what had been the greatest flood in our history in 1882, which was later said to be a heavy dew in comparison to the 1927 overflow. This flood of 1882 inundated different parts of the same section hit by the 1927 flood. It is said that in 1796, a flood of similar nature to that of 1927 did engulf practically all the same country in much the same manner. The flood waters of 1927 found the old channel of the Red River.

As early as April, Iberians were cooperating with other state groups to try to protect the land. Going to Plaquemine for a meeting were the President of the Police Jury Clet Girard, Mayor Ed LaSalle, P. A. Landry, Fred Patout, Emile Vuillemot, and Marcus DeBlanc. Some parts of Iberia Parish were already under water, but the worst was yet to come.

Complying with the request of the American Red Cross, the Iberia Chapter through its chairman, Lloyd Porter, assisted by members of the Chamber of Commerce, received donations amounting to $2,033.56 during the first week of May. Iberia Parish had been assessed $1,400. Later, more was given as needs increased.

On Monday, May 16, a joint meeting of the American Red Cross and Chamber of Commerce was held to name the following committees: transportation—Francis Voorhies, E. H. Buffington, C. Arthur Provost, and F. G. Patout; food—Leon Minvielle, George Germany, and John O. Bonin; sanitation — Dr. J. W. Sanders, Ed L. Estorge, and John R. Taylor; camp—P. R. Burke, and Sylvio Brousard. L. G. Porter was chairman of all committees.

There were many days of strenuous activity, during which people were moved from the Loreauville section, which was in the path of the flood. Farmers to the west and southwest of

New Iberia, under the leadership of Ulysse and Leon Landry, assisted by Theo David, Joe Segura, Evrard Broussard, Arvilien Segura, Paul Segura, and the Robichaux brothers, worked together to hold back the onrushing waters from Spanish Lake. For days and nights without rest, they filled the culverts along the highway and built levees across all the low places leading into the lake as far down as the Gabriel Darby property. Spanish Lake filled up. Panic stricken people left by car and train. It was estimated that on this first day of exodus a thousand people left, eighty per cent of them Negroes. All night Tuesday, May 24, the flood waters were inundating St. Martinville. The public road from there to New Iberia was flooded, and by midnight all lands in front of the Wyche home were submerged. By daylight the area between Bayou Teche and Spanish Lake was filled completely. The water from the lake began to rush toward New Iberia with a frightening, rumbling roar that could be heard about a half hour before the water was seen. Although the homes on the "hill" were not flooded, within a short time there was about two feet of water in Louis Lalland's store on Jane Street near the Missouri Pacific railroad track. Then the flood was momentarily stopped. The embankments of the Missouri Pacific tracks on the north and of the Southern Pacific track on the west were enough to hold back the force of the water which began to trickle in. These embankments probably saved many homes from much damage. Thousands went to see the sight. On Thursday, New Iberia began to be submerged; and the water rose until Friday night, when it remained at one stage overnight. The following morning a slight recession was perceptible. The waters had spread from Port Barre over a hundred miles from New Iberia, to Franklin, about thirty miles down the bayou from New Iberia.

About noon Friday the Powerhouse became submerged, completely paralyzing the sewerage system and temporarily cutting off the light and power system. At once the State Board of Health sent out engineers, and the electric current was turned on about 10 A. M. Sunday.

There was a rise of twenty and a half feet in the Teche waters. From Thursday, May 26, to 6 A. M. the next morning, the bayou rose seven and a half feet. When the water started to recede, it went down almost as quickly. However, some homes and industries along the bayou banks were under water for about a month. As far back as Marie Street many yards had as much as six feet of water, and homes along the east bayou bank had as much as six to eight feet of water inside.

The first casualty noted was the drowning, May 28, of Ralph Lee, a Negro, in the canal (now filled up) on Ann Street, where he lived.

An alligator four feet, five inches long was discovered by children playing in the yard of Mrs. Walter Nereaux. It was killed by a fourteen year old boy, Webster Lusk. A larger alligator was later seen in the same area.

The approach on the east end of the bridge on Bridge Street was torn away by a government boat, the *Vermilion*, on May 28, to open a clear path for navigation.

Help and cooperation during this time of trouble were remarkable. The American Red Cross, National Guard, State Flood Relief Administration, all organized groups, and individuals coordinated their efforts. Assistance from sister towns and nearly every nearby town in the state as well as from Texas was given.

Many extra trains were run, free of cost, by the Missouri Pacific and Southern Pacific Lines to move refugees and live stock to safety. On special trains came Texas cowboys and their steeds to round up thousands of head of cattle. F. C. Quereau told of having seen these Texas cowboys save 225 cattle which had been washed by the swift current into a tangle of wires. It was impossible to use boats in the strong current so the cowboys went in with wire cutters in a melee of bawling cattle and screaming horses. They cut wires and untangled some of the animals. Then a cow was grasped by the tail and steered to high ground, and all the cattle that had been released followed. This procedure was repeated until all living animals had been saved. Texas paid for the rescue work done by the cowboys, while the men continually risked their lives.

A great many of our own young men went for four days and nights, never removing their shoes, to rescue people from the east side of the bayou. Many women, too, rendered invaluable aid through the Red Cross and other organizations.

Dr. Oscar Dowling, the Parish and City Health Officer, asked Dr. W. F. Carstens to serve as medical and sanitary officer for the homeless. At first the white refugees were housed in the New Iberia High School and the colored, at Howe Institute. The doctors of the city were asked to serve as staff members for the two groups. Katherine Avery, sent here by the State Board of Health, was appointed head nurse at the high school; and Miss Beck, a Red Cross nurse, was at Howe Institute. When Dr. Carstens injured his shoulder, Dr. J. W. Sanders took over his duties.

Camps were established on high ground on the banks of Spanish Lake between Segura and Burke stations after New Iberia was inundated. Roy Camp on the Atkinson place was for the white people; and McGlade Camp, under Rev. Father McGlade, on the old Pharr plantation, was for the colored. At the time of moving the camps from the town, all patients had been sent to Lafayette. Then the Atkinson home was set up as a sanitarium.

On June 9, Secretary of Commerce Herbert Hoover, met in New Iberia with the chairman of the Rehabilitation Committee, L. G. Porter, and the members P. R. Burke, Ed L. Estorge, and E. A. McIlhenny. Each ward had a representative to direct the clean-up work. The state and local Boards of Health inspected every yard.

The volunteer chairman and vice-chairman of the New Iberia Chapter of the American Red Cross, Mrs. Daniel D. Avery and Mrs. John R. Taylor, distributed clothing to the needy in camp and then set up headquarters in the Elks home to continue the work for any other needy people.

On July 15, the camps were formally closed, and the Red Cross workers either returned home or engaged in other fields of activity. Bradley Kelly, a national representative of the Red Cross who had given invaluable service in the parish, returned to his home in New York and was replaced by H. A. Green, another national representative who was to help the local Chapter as long as necessary.

The ration store and warehouse were moved into the Lewald building on Main and French Streets, while the clothing department was moved to Loreauville under the supervision of Mrs. George Germany.

About the middle of July, the highway between St. Martinville and New Iberia was opened to traffic.

Jeanerette practically escaped the flood waters because of the many outlets to the gulf between New Iberia and that city. Only the homes and industries along the bayou were flooded.

* * * * * *

The early farmers in Iberia Parish found a variety of lands. Much of the land was bottom or marsh land and had to be drained. The water on the open prairie seemed undetermined as to which way to flow. The cultivated lands were chiefly along the Teche, as the higher ground was to be found there. Some parts of the parish are even higher than along the Teche. These rolling uplands are the islands—Petite Anse or Avery, Grand Cote or Weeks, Orange Island or Jefferson, and Cote Blanche. A tract of good tillable land lying to the south and west of New Iberia is Prairie au Large. It has a width of about six miles and the fertility common to the lands of the parish.

The first cash crops in this section were indigo and cotton; crops for home consumption were rice and tobacco. Before the end of the eighteenth century, indigo lost importance, as insects were destroying it. Sugar cane began to replace indigo.

Cotton cultivation was started early in Louisiana. At least as early as 1722 some cotton was grown and used by the colonists. The labor in the cotton fields, which often lasted from August to February, was the most continuous of all. The cold damp mornings of the winter months made cotton-picking quite unpleasant.

The year 1867 was a lean year for crops. No cotton was made because of a plague of caterpillars, which swarmed the countryside, devouring everything before them, even to the foliage in the trees of the woods. Adding to the desolation of destruction was a solid network of web, which hung from tree to tree. This destruction by caterpillars was repeated on other occasions, one being in the early 1880's.

In the vicinity of Loreauville there were many small cotton planters. Some sugar planters, who were discouraged with the scarcity of laborers and the low price of sugar, followed the cotton planters and turned to cotton. In the 1870 census 1,297 bales of cotton are recorded for Iberia Parish. A total of 7,443 acres of land was planted in cotton in 1879; 2,482 bales were produced. The cotton acreage had increased in 1890 to 14,198 acres. That year 5,056 bales were produced, and 2,022 tons of cotton seed sold at a value of $20,022.

By 1900 the cotton acreage had dropped to 7,121, with 3,948 commercial bales reported by the farmers. This drop in the amount of land planted in cotton was not indicative of the amount of land being cultivated: the total number of acres of cultivated land in 1880 had risen to 129,403. This total increased to 132,388 acres in 1890, and to 149,577 acres in 1900. Sugar cane was surely taking the place of cotton.

The change from cotton to sugar cane gave much more work during the harvest, or "rolling season." Besides the field work there was the work at the sugar mill, which required wood cutting and cording and the night watches, or "tours." Yet, unlike cotton picking, the *roulaison* had many opportunities for adding pleasure to work. The workers sang and joked as they kept busy. They enjoyed chewing sugar cane, drinking hot juice, and eating the molasses or sugar in its various stages.

The local newspapers often published comments on the condition of the crops. In deploring the June rains in 1871, one newspaper stated that, although the season had opened unusually early and had given the best promise since the war, the late cold spells followed by the rain had held back the cultivation and growth of the cane and that in all probability the crop would not mature any earlier than usual. In July of the same year, a specimen of sugar cane, six feet tall, was brought to the editor of the newspaper. It contained sixteen joints and weighed three and three-fourths pounds. In August a seven-foot cane with sixteen red joints was brought in to the office of the *Louisiana Sugar Bowl*.

But the yield from the cane crop was not good in 1871. On a plantation between New Iberia and Jeanerette, thirty-five acres had been worked, and it was expected to yield about an average of one hogshead (1125 weight) of sugar to an arpent. The drought in the spring and then the heavy rains had damaged the crops. No profit was expected on the crop-grinding that year. On another plantation near Jeanerette, the same season, the labor for taking off the cane for three hogsheads of

Above—Sugar Plantation on the Bayou Teche, Louisiana

Below—A Sugar House Along the Teche

"The finest sugar plantations meet the eye at frequent intervals, and every bend of the river discloses new scenes of agricultural beauty and thrift."

Sketches by A. R. Waud in Harper's Weekly, December 8, 1866. (From the collection of Leonard V. Huber of New Orleans) sugar amounted to $218. To add to the woes of the farmer, came a freeze and difficulty in obtaining fuel. This planter was so disgusted that he asserted he would never again cultivate cane.

In the early 1870's the parish had not yet recovered from the effects of the Civil War. Mention is made on several occasions of trying out the machinery in the sugar mills which had been damaged and idle. One planter produced 150 hogsheads of sugar and yet did not meet expenses. His mill had remained unused since the war until the past season, 1871-1872, and no doubt needed many repairs.

There is a record of a plantation owned by a Mr. Stevens, on which a fine crop of sugar was made. Five hands were employed to work about fifty acres in cane. The cane from forty-three of the acres produced fifty-six hogsheads of sugar. To this was added the information that three hundred barrels of corn were also produced on this farm, and all with the use of only six mules.

In the fall of the following year the opinion of the planters was that the sugar crop in Iberia Parish would be considerably larger than the last unless the weather should become unfavorable and cause the cane to freeze or sour.

The section of the parish at Fausse Pointe around the outer portion of the bend of the Teche above New Iberia was principally prairie. The inside portion, rich and above overflow, produced to the acre large quantities of a superior quality of sugar. Furthermore the facilities for shipment were considered to be of the best.

Usually sugar planters were manufacturers as well as producers. It was predicted in 1885 that this system would come to an end, as a few bad years caused too great a loss to be borne by one person. Besides, a small sugar house, with imperfect machinery, entailed a loss of from twenty to fifty per cent of what the gross value of what an acre of cane should be.

After the Civil War and before 1900, one of the plantations in the parish, the Weeks Plantation, was described as being in a fine condition and well cultivated. The soil was very fertile, a fact which contributed to its productiveness. The plantation had all the buildings and improvements of the most successful sugar estate in the district. There was a large brick sugar house with a slate roof. The sugar mill had a capacity to make six to eight hundred hogsheads of sugar yearly.

In 1870 the cane production for Iberia Parish was 1,856 hogsheads of sugar and 102,495 gallons of molasses. In 1879 a total of 6,509 acres were planted in cane, with a yield of 6,399 hogsheads of sugar and 297,654 gallons of molasses. The increase in acreage for sugar cane, by 1890, was great, and 12,016 acres were planted, with the result that 11,182,350 pounds of sugar and 445,756 gallons of molasses were produced. In 1899 in its value of sugar cane and cane products Iberia Parish ranked ninth in the state. The sugar produced was 6,214,800 pounds, with a value of $9,028; and 57,932 gallons of sirup, valued at $13,888.

Besides sugar cane there were some other important crops. In 1870, 115,843 bushels of corn were produced, 12,500 pounds of rice, 135 bushels of Irish potatoes, and 12,414 bushels of sweet potatoes. In 1900 farmers harvested 564,670 bushels of corn, 5,580 bushels of Irish potatoes, and 83,931 bushels of sweet potatoes. The same year the value of all orchard products was $1,121. There were 1,276 pecan trees in the parish, which produced 51,900 pounds of nuts.

In 1896 Oscar Darby experimented in coffee culture. He grew a few plants and saved sufficient seed to plant a row one and one-half arpents long. Although the coffee was reported growing well, Mr. Darby's attempt never amounted to more than an experiment.

From seed sent him by Senator Caffery in Washington, Ozeme Jacob produced in his garden a three-pound plug of tobacco. It was of the Havana Round Leaf variety. Jacob expected fifteen pounds of fine quality tobacco from this crop and expected to plant more tobacco the following year. This project did not prove successful.

For many years before the Civil War, farms were becoming princely estates. The more successful a farmer was, the more slaves he bought; then he added to his acreage. A squeezing process was often used to make a small farmer sell. Often one or two heirs in a family would buy out the portion of the other heirs in order to keep the farm and slaves as one large holding.

After the Civil War there was, in many instances, a change to share cropping. Some system had to be worked out by which the laborers and landowners could live together. There were many ex-slaves and landless whites needing work, and the landowner had to set up some way of getting his land worked with the use of as little cash as possible. Since most of the cash used by the planters was borrowed, it was necessary that cash crops be planted. The tenant farm seemed to be the answer. The landowners risked losing their farms, and the tenant not only had to share the risk of farming but was faced, in many instances, with a continued low standard of living. The more a tenant was able to supply himself with farm animals and implements, the more he was able to profit from his work.

The *Louisiana Sugar Bowl* remarks that most successful planters were those who worked on the share-system. The planter who was on his own had to hire men, pay overseers, and meet many other expenses. On a share-system plantation near Jeanerette, six working men expected to make about forty hogsheads of sugar. The planter received two-thirds of the sugar, a seemingly beneficial amount. On another plantation in the vicinity of Loreauville, a number of houses were being erected on three sides of the place, to be used later for share croppers.

The census shows that in 1880 there were 753 farms cultivated by the owners, 124 rented for a fixed money rental, and 477 rented for a share of the products. In 1890, 723 farms were cultivated by the owners, fifty-nine rented for a fixed money value, and 176 to be worked on shares. The average size of the farms was 138 acres. By 1900 this average size had decreased to 81.8 acres. In that year the farms were worked by 931 owners, twenty-nine part owners, two owners and tenants, twenty managers, 259 cash tenants, and 587 share tenants.

From the beginning of the settlement, stock raising was the standby of the colonists and farmers; it continued to be so at the time of and after the Louisiana Purchase. In the early 1870's stock raising was considered more profitable than planting. At this time there was a movement for raising blooded cattle for market. Propagating a good strain of animals, which brought a higher market price, cost no more than raising ordinary cattle. Because of the superior grazing throughout the year,

Iberia Parish was especially suited for stock raising. New Orleans provided a good market for livestock and dairy products; this market served the area as another advantage for stock raising. All along the bayou there were cattle pens with facilities for shipping

The value of all livestock in 1870 amounted to $142,746. There were 1,834 milch cows, 711 working oxen, and 3,998 other cattle. By 1880 this number had increased to more than double, as then there was a total of 13,341 animals. This trend was reversed, however, in 1890, when the number of cattle fell to 12,827. The decrease in cattle continued in 1900, when a total of only 8,175 was reported in the census. These decreases were caused chiefly by an epidemic of various diseases in 1885, and of charbon in 1898. However, the value of livestock had increased to $734,419. The total value of all dairy products was $91,438. The value of the products consumed on the farms was $72,545.

In the year 1871 a pound was established in each ward for hogs at large and all unbranded animals found in the district. Then, in 1873, the Police Jury declared that the owners of animals causing damage to property were responsible and must fence in the animals. Later the same year this ordinance was postponed for enforcement until June, 1874.

The trouble with unfenced animals seemed to continue, as, in 1880, another ordinance was passed by the Police Jury. By this ruling persons owning no lands had the right to keep at large no more than twelve head of horses, cattle and sheep collectively. Any greater number of these animals had to be kept enclosed. In 1894 the Board of Trustees passed an ordinance prohibiting the roaming of cattle within the limits of the corporation of New Iberia.

Horses and mules were necessary on the farm and were also raised for the market. In 1870 there were 1,271 horses and 834 mules and asses. These had greatly increased in number by 1880. Their total, by 1890, had dropped, but by 1900 it had risen again to 3,871 horses and 4,816 mules, asses, and burros.

As they cost little or nothing, hogs were of considerable profit and advantage on a sugar plantation. They prevented waste by consuming various kinds of refuse materials. In 1879 a twenty-seven months old hog, raised in the parish, was killed and weighed 812 pounds when clean. There were 1,569 swine in 1870, and 9,985 in 1900.

Although sheep were raised in Iberia Parish, they were not as numerous and important as other livestock. In 1870 there were 3,511 sheep on the farms in the parish. About the same number were held in 1880, but by 1890 there were only 1,160. As time went on fewer sheep were raised, so that by 1900 there were only 916. These produced 2,160 pounds of wool.

Of course, the people of Iberia Parish, like other rural people, raised chickens and other fowl. Exclusive of the spring hatching there were, in June, 1880, 75,897 fowl. Although the number of fowl had not increased in 1890, the egg production had. By 1900 there was a large increase in the number of fowl. Chickens and guinea fowl numbered 104,387; turkeys 1,392; geese 1,838; and ducks 3,763. The value of all this poultry on hand was $28,968.

Another rural production was honey from domestic bees. From one hundred pounds of honey produced in 1879 there was an increase of 4,320 pounds in 1890, and 12,860 pounds in 1899. The wax obtained in 1899 amounted to 160 pounds. In 1900 the bees were valued at $655.

The farmers established organizations by which they benefited: in knowledge of agriculture, in obtaining better seed, and in increasing their produce. The old agrarian organization, the Farmers' Union, was reorganized into the Farmers' Alliance. One instance of cooperation was the farmers' institute organized by the commissioner of agriculture, J. G. Lee, in the summer of 1897. One of the meetings was an all-day session and was presided over by W. R. Farmer. E. S. Broussard acted as secretary. Today the organizations which help farmers in the parish are the Iberia Cattlemen's Association and the Iberia Parish Farm Bureau. The cane growers belong to the American Sugar Cane League which is a state organization made up of the cane-belt parishes.

By hard work the rural people of Iberia Parish in varying degrees, developed the land. The more fortunate were able to have luxuries; but as usual, many, through no fault of their own, only managed to make a living.

CHAPTER IV

THE TOWNS AND THE PEOPLE

When the Spaniards under Bouligny came to what is now Iberia Parish, they called their settlement Nueva Iberia. Later the place was known as New Town. Still later it was incorporated under the title of the "Town of Iberia." The name "New Iberia" came into official existence with Act. No. 160, passed by the Louisiana Legislature and approved April 24, 1847.

Although the names "Iberia" and "Iberian" are used in reference to ancient people other than the Spanish, the name of the town is derived from inhabitants of ancient time who lived at the mouth of the Iberus (Ebro) River in Spain. "Iberia" was an ancient name for Spain.

On Darby's *Map of Louisiana (1816-17)*, there is shown a settlement called New Iberia. As far back as 1785 a census reports New Iberia as having a population of 125; by 1788 this number had grown to 190. The 1848 population of New Iberia was 300.

William Darby, a traveler-writer, prophesied that, if elegance of site or beauty of prospect could bestow prosperity upon a town, none could be superior to New Iberia. The town, for instance, was situated much more favorably for commerce than St. Martinville. However, Darby warned that even these advantages would be of small avail, as long as the people insisted upon trading directly with New Orleans. Another traveler, Timothy Flint, was of the opinion that New Iberia would eventually become a place of importance.

Many instances of references to a settlement at New Iberia can be found in existing archives. In the Weeks Papers, Mary C. Weeks, in 1802, referred to New Town. In 1820, the heading of a letter was "Novia Iberia." In 1821, the names New Iberia and Nova Iberia appeared. Obviously then, New Iberia was settled and known for many years before it was incorporated.

Frederick H. Duperier had acquired, by the middle 1820's,

Main Street, New Iberia, 1863

Main Street, New Iberia, 1910

Main Street, New Iberia, 1961

from the Henry Pintard Succession, land two and one-half arpents front, on the west side of the bayou, by a depth of forty arpents and two and one-half arpents on the east side of the bayou by a depth limited by the same bayou which made a bend.

In 1835 Frederick H. Duperier, at the suggestion of two of his personal friends, had the land surveyed for the Town of Iberia. Tradition says a Mr. Dow was the surveyor.[1] This section was laid out between Iberia Street and Corinne Street and extended back from the banks of the Teche to the property owned by the late Thomas Johnson. At this time a plot of ground was reserved on St. Peter Street for a church. The plot reserved was donated in 1836 by Frederick Duperier to a board of directors authorized to construct a Catholic Church on the land.

The charter for the Town of Iberia in the parish of St. Martin was approved by the Legislature on March 13, 1839, as Act. No. 16.[2] This charter defined the town limits. Five free holders, residents of the town, were to constitute the "Trustees of the Town of Iberia." One of this group was selected by the members to act as president. Tax money, not to exceed $200 a year, could be raised to be used for the improvement and police of the town. If more money than specified was needed, it could be raised by having the president of the board of trustees call a special election with five days advance notice, for a vote of approval by the majority of the votes. Regulations for elections and the duties of the officers were stated.

The town's charter was amended in 1847, and the name of the village was changed to New Iberia. Also the amount of taxes it was allowed to collect was changed from $200 to $500 per annum. In 1855 the amended charter allowed the taxation to be increased to $1,000. Again in 1860 and 1868 the charter was amended. The 1868 charter was amended chiefly to recognize the rights of the Negroes after their emancipation. In this charter the city limits were again extended, including ten acres on the east side of the bayou; and the limits of revenue were abolished, provided the amount imposed and collected did not

---

[1]It is recorded in the State Land Office that the lands in this township were surveyed by Jacob McMichael in 1829, and resurveyed partly by A. L. Fields in 1839, and by Boyd and Warren in 1845-1848.
[2]Frederick H. Duperier died March 15, 1839.

— 49 —

exceed the parish tax in one year. The number of trustees was increased from five to seven.

At a later date, about the early 1870's, New Iberia had a mayor. This government was altered in the 1920's to a commission form of government, with a mayor, a commissioner of finances, and a commissioner of public property. This type of government did not prove popular with the people, and New Iberia returned to a mayor and trustees. In time there were ten trustees. To ease the work of the administration, the voters, in 1950, decided to divide the city into six districts, with one alderman or trustee for each district.

In a letter written in 1838, New Iberia, is described as "a very pretty place with well built houses, several stores, a post office, bank, hotels, large distillery, church, and public school."

A severe epidemic of yellow fever struck New Iberia the year the town was incorporated (1839). Practically every family was affected by the horrible disease. Nearly one-half of the population died during this epidemic.

This 1839 epidemic was started as a result of the shipping here for burial the body of Dr. Raphael W. Smith, who had resided in New Iberia but had later moved to Plaquemine, where he died of the fever. He was the brother of Dr. Leonard J. Smith of New Iberia.

There is a story about this. The Smith body was put off at the Smith plantation, (which later became the property of Hopkins then of the Lourd family,) in a metal case filled with rum and was left in the sugar house awaiting interment. An idiotic Negro on Dr. Smith's plantation smelled the rum from afar as it leaked out. Watching his chance, the Negro drank enough of the rum to become drunk. Needless to say, he was "fever-proof."

One of the first victims of the dread disease was Dr. Neal, a leading physician of the town. Dr. Abby was also stricken. He was cared for by Felicité, a brave and kind colored woman who became very well known because of her ministrations to both white and black sufferers. Felicité was assisted in this work of mercy by Mrs. Maximilien Decuir, Mrs. David Hayes, Mrs. Barron Bayard, and Mrs. Don Louis Broussard. Felicité was not forgotten; and at her death, in 1852, her body lay in state at the home of her former master, Frederick Duperier, while hundreds of people of both races paid their last respects to her.

Asiatic cholera struck several plantations along the Teche in 1848. One of these places was the plantation of Mrs. Dubuclet. When the manager of the plantation, Simonette LeBlanc,[3] noticed the disease among the slaves, he tried to escape the plague by going to Lake Simonette. The plague, however, struck his family after he was at Lake Simonette. When Dr. Wells went to care for the family, the doctor contracted the disease.

There were succeeding epidemics of yellow fever several of which were mild in New Iberia (1852, 1854, 1878, 1897, and 1898) but one of which was sufficiently severe to reduce the population considerably. In the 1867 epidemic, nearly every other house was struck by the terror. There were 280 deaths in New Iberia. Dr. Alfred Duperier was the only physician who escaped. Physicians from New Orleans came out to assist him.[4]

In August, 1878, the lines of quarantine were extended beyond the corporate limits of New Iberia. All places in the parish infected by the disease were quarantined. No dry goods or any object thought to communicate the disease or any persons coming from an infected area were allowed to enter the district.

The Police Jury minutes for September, 1878, show that a Board of Health for the parish was created, composed of the Board of Health of New Iberia and one citizen from each ward. In 1883, the Board of Trustees became a Board of Health and decided all health questions until September, 1898, when both the Police Jury and City Council of New Iberia appointed Boards of Health for the parish and town.

---

[3]After Simon White, a northerner, settled here and married an Acadian his name was translated to LeBlanc. Lake Simonette near Jefferson Island bears the name of his son, Simonette.

[4]Dr. Solenge of Province Dauphine, France, may have been the first doctor to settle in what is now Iberia Parish. He was a highly educated physician, who was married to a Miss Pellerin, an invalid, who had inherited a large number of slaves. These slaves became possessed with the idea that Dr. Solenge was treating his wife in a way that would slowly bring on her death. One stormy night, as he was returning from a call, he was shot and killed. A close relative of Mrs. Solenge had the slaves drawn up in a line; and while slowly walking along the line, occasionally told a slave to step aside. Seven slaves were taken out of line, and five of these confessed to the murder. These guilty slaves were executed on the spot where Dr. Solenge had been killed.

As early as 1885, there was a medical society for this area. The Attakapas Medical Association met in New Iberia in May, 1885. The May meeting was held regularly in New Iberia, and the December meeting was held at any convenient place. Press comments show that the State Medical Society was planning to hold its 1886 meeting in New Iberia.

The Attakapas Sanitarium was ready for service in January, 1899. Dr. T. J. Woolf opened the infirmary to all invalids except those with infectious diseases. The place could be used by any reputable physician in the city.

To increase sanitation daily garbage collection, under the direction of the municipal government, began October 7, 1899. A mule and cart were used for this purpose.

Iberia Parish's first public health nurse was Miss Katherine Avery. She helped to organize the Iberia Parish Health Unit in 1928, the New Iberia Tuberculosis Association, and the Crippled Children's Clinic.

As long as New Iberia was in Attakapas District or St. Martin Parish, there were no resident lawyers in the town. Probably the first lawyer to live in New Iberia was Joseph A. Breaux. He was named Chief Justice of the Supreme Court of Louisiana in 1890. At the time of his appointment, he was the State Superintendent of Education. The next lawyer to come to New Iberia was Robert Perry, who became a judge of the circuit court. The first District Judge for Iberia Parish was Frederick Gates, who was also a lawyer. Emmanuel J. Etie was the first Parish Judge of Iberia.

When most of the people of the state and the nation were strongly Democrats, most of the people of Iberia were Whigs. In 1853 the "Know Nothing" party reached New Iberia and caused much hard feeling. This feeling dissipated with the coming of the Republican party. During the war between the states, civil authority was suspended and was replaced by military authority. No records for this period are in existence, if any were kept, and those prior to the war were destroyed. The first existing minutes for the Board of Trustees in New Iberia is dated July 7, 1868. E. J. Etie was president of the Board at the time.

After Louisiana was readmitted to the union in 1868, there followed a period of fraud, corruption, and malversation of public funds. During this time Dominique Ulger "Gachon" Broussard and James L. Burke were the Democratic leaders. Theodore Fontelieu was leader of the Republicans and did much to get the vote of the Negro. In 1871 New Iberia had a seven-member Board of Trustees, which served for a term of one year and had executive, legislative, and administrative powers.

Political conditions were not too bad in Iberia Parish until 1872, when the radical element took over. Then the editor of the *Sugar Bowl* complained that whenever a colored person committed a crime grievous enough to send a white man to the penitentiary, the colored person was usually either excused because of his ignorance of right from wrong or given a trivial punishment. In the early 1870's there was only a semblance of law and order. There was rioting among Negroes, street fights, open gambling, shootings, and murders. The government was influenced by the Freedmen's Bureau and decisions were made to favor the Republicans.

Negroes refused to work except for exorbitant wages. In January, 1874, the Negroes, under the direction of Representative Henry Demas, held a mass meeting at the Court House to plan a strike. The wage of $13.00 a month plus food, clothing and shelter, fixed by Gen Banks, had been raised by competition of the planters to $25.00. The drop in production, high taxes, and exhausted savings had resulted in a lowering of wages. A resolution to stop work was made at this meeting. (Strange to say, the Negro, when working for himself, was not as efficient as when he worked as a slave.)

During the radical administration of Governor William Pitt Kellogg, 1873-1877, Marcel Boutte, the only colored man who ever sat on the Board of Trustees, was elected. New Iberia also had a Negro constable, and a Negro city judge by the name of Simon. There were also two colored postmasters in New Iberia— Samuel Wakefield then Charles Decuir.

For the purpose of wresting the government from the carpetbaggers and scalawags, mass meetings were held in New Iberia, as they were throughout the state. White Leagues were formed in many places. These different clubs were represented at meetings of the Central Committee of Iberia Parish. The purpose of these clubs was to regain white supremacy. The White League opposed fraudulent registration, campaigned for all whites to register, and attempted to protect and defend the colored people who were being duped by the carpetbaggers. In Iberia Parish the "White Camelia" was under the command of Robert S. Perry.

J. Y. Gilmore, editor of the *Sugar Bowl* in 1874, was involved in five libel suits; but, in spite of this, he continued to speak for honest government.

The greatest struggle up to 1878 was directed at taking the government from the control of the Republicans. A democratic Conservative Convention was held in New Iberia, with colored people attending. In July of the same year an appeal was made to all classes and races for honest officials. To effect a concerted movement to defeat the radicals, Robert S. Perry, Chairman of the Democratic Conservative Parish Executive Committee, attempted to bring all who were against radicalism under Conservative Democracy. A mass meeting was held with the object of electing delegates to the State Nominating Convention in Baton Rouge and to recognize the Democratic Conservative Party in Iberia Parish.

The Iberia Guards, a local unit similar to the National Guards, was organized as a rallying point for maintaining order. A cavalry company, the Regulators, was soon after organized with C. T. Cade as captain. The Regulators was at first a secret organization which rode at night, hooded, as did the Ku Klux Klan.

The rancor of the political groups culminated in the Battle of Loreauville on Sunday, November 1, 1884. The Republicans of the parish were holding a political meeting. Several good Democrats attended the meeting, among them Captain Bell and Joseph Guilfoux. The *Times-Democrat,* a newspaper published in New Orleans, reported that the first shot at Guilfoux was fired by a Negro. The shooting became general, and both Bell and Guilfoux were killed before being able to defend themselves. It was not definitely known how many were killed that day. The parish priest and other cool heads helped to restore order to the community.

With the aid of the state militia, in 1884, the Democrats regained control of the parish. Some of the elected officials were P. A. Veazey, Sheriff; Fred Gates, District Judge; and Adolph

Wakefield, a Negro who had joined the Democrats, Clerk of Court. In May, 1885, the Police Jury reported irregularities in the entries of the Clerk of Court.

Fontelieu continued to be the leader of the opposition, and there continued to be trouble between the political factions, especially at election time. The 1884 elections were contested by Fontelieu. The records of these elections with other public archives were said to have been stolen from the Iberia Parish Court House. These papers later turned up at Franklin in the possession of Fontelieu's attorneys, one of whom was Fontelieu's son. The attorneys were arrested for being in possession of papers stolen from the Iberia Parish Court House. A special term of Court was ordered by Judge Goode, but on the appointed day the demonstration by Fontelieu's friends was so violent that his attorneys advised a postponement of the trial. Later the attorneys in possession of the stolen papers were found guilty, and eventually Fontelieu lost his suit.

Fontelieu was a candidate for District Judge in 1888. On election day the Iberia Guards, under their captain, A. C. Burkhart, were mobilized. The balloting was orderly except that, when a Negro attempted to vote, he was forcefully persuaded not to do so. The commissioners suggested counting the votes in the upstairs court room away from the crowd. Fontelieu's brother, his representative, agreed, provided that he carry the ballot box. When they were about half way, a pistol was fired and the lamp blown out. Fontelieu tripped and rolled down the steps, dropping the ballot box. When the ballots were counted, James E. Mouton was elected District Judge by a large majority.

Negroes continued to vote for many years, but gradually they were persuaded to stay away from the polls. The persuasion was usually peaceful, but on occasion force was resorted to by the whites who were again in control. In recent years the Negro has regained the privilege of suffrage.

For many years schools were closed on election day, and children kept at home away from any possible disturbance.

Since the Republicans were not able to carry the vote in the national elections, each political faction in New Iberia tried to gain control of the Democratic Party. There was no need to have two parties, and for this reason the Parish Executive Committee was reorganized in 1890.

The Socialist Party was organized in New Iberia in October, 1904. One of the national organizers, John M. Ray, came to address the meeting.

* * * * * *

When the parish of Iberia was formed, New Iberia was made the parish seat. The quarters in which the Police Jury met and conducted its business were, for a time, temporary. In the book of Original Conveyances, under entry No. 17, it is recorded that on January 7, 1869, Louis Miguez leased to Daniel D. Avery, as president of the Police Jury, the upper story of a brick and frame building situated on Main Street. The Police Jury was also to have the use of water out of the brick cistern in the rear of the brick building. The partitions were to be removed by the leaseholder and the building returned in good condition. The yearly rent was $800, payable quarterly. In the minutes of August, 1870, $200 for three months' rent was ordered paid to Louis Miguez. These temporary quarters were burned in 1870 and other temporary buildings were used until the first permanent building was finished in 1884.

Because of the fire, no Police Jury minutes are in existence previous to the ones of August 2, 1870. These first minutes tell of plans to construct a temporary courthouse and offices. Apparently this temporary courthouse was not built, for in the October minutes, there is a record of the Police Jury's acceptance of an offer made by P. A. Veazey, which offer proposed to rent to the Parish, as a courthouse, the upper story of the brick building then in the course of erection on Main Street. The building was to be ready for occupancy on January 1, 1871.

The proceedings of the Police Jury of December 15, 1877, show that the State General Assembly was asked to enact a law authorizing the Police Jury of Iberia Parish to contract a debt by negotiating a loan of $15,000. This sum was to be used for building a Courthouse and jail in New Iberia. The same law would authorize a tax of not more than five mills on assessments for the years 1878 through 1882. On February 2, 1882, a report was made at the Police Jury meeting by the president, D. U. Broussard, that the purchase of a Courthouse lot had been completed with Messrs. Taylor and DeValcourt. The lot was bought for $4,000. The first payment of $1,000 in cash was made at this time. The rest was to be made in six equal installments of $500 each, payable yearly with eight per cent interest per annum from date, with the right of the Police Jury to take up any or all of its notes at any time it might think proper.

In 1884 the Police Jury appointed a committee composed of Fred Gates, J. A. Lee, C. T. Cade, and William R. Burke to take charge of the Courthouse construction. The committee chose W. R. Burke as superintendent of construction. This committee in June, 1885, turned in a report of the work done, including a list of all expenses, and requested that the committee be discharged The total cost of the new brick Courthouse amounted to $22,447.70.

With the passing of time, the parish outgrew its Courthouse; and a handsome Courthouse was completed in April, 1940, at a cost of a half million dollars.

New Iberia grew from a population of 1,472 in 1870 to 6,815 in 1900. Naturally, this period of growth in population went along with improvements for the town. In 1851, the first bridge across the Teche in New Iberia had been built and Bridge Street was opened. A quotation from the New Iberia *Democrat* of May 24, 1890, tells that the material for the construction of the iron bridge across Bayou Teche had arrived and that, as soon as conditions were favorable, the work was to begin. The report stated further that arrangements had already been made for a ferry boat to be used during this period of construction.

The September 13, 1890 edition of the paper announced that the handsome iron bridge was "now open to travelers" and added that a few finishing touches were to be made before the corporation and parish authorities would accept it. Finally November 1, 1890, at two o'clock, a joint committee accepted the bridge. The building of this bridge was another piece of engineering work of which the Iberians were proud.

This first iron bridge has been replaced by a modern one and two other bridges have also been constructed for traffic across the Teche within the corporate limits of New Iberia.

Common usage gave names to the different sections or suburbs of New Iberia. In 1885 a section known as Georgetown extended west from Hopkins Street. Leesburg was located to the east; Opelousas was still another section; and Coopersville was across the bayou. It is a tradition that the first home that was built on the east side of Bayou Teche was that of Frederick Duperier. In 1843 Jacques Lamperez built in that section. This house still stands on the corner of Front and Johnson Streets. In 1846 Jean Marie bought property and built near the road to the ferry. About the middle of the nineteenth century the Duperier-Hebert home was constructed. This home is now a part of Dauterive Hospital.

Many destructive fires occurred in New Iberia. On June 20, 1870, Main Street, on both sides, was burned from Bridge Street eastward to the city limits. Over thirty houses were destroyed. The people were panic stricken, as the town had no fire protection.

After many disastrous fires and much campaigning by the newspaper editors, a fire-fighting organization was formed in 1868. Benefit entertainments were held from time to time in order to raise money for volunteer companies. An example of this was the excursion from New Iberia to Alexandria, sponsored by Fire Company No. 1. Seven hundred to eight hundred people took part and a profit of $667.95 was made.

In the 1880's the town organized two steam engine companies and one hook and ladder company.

After a series of fires in 1890, two horses were bought by one of the fire companies to pull the hand engine around. The horses were rented to the express company; but this didn't prove successful, as the horses sometimes mistook the train bell for the fire signal. On one occasion, not being securely tied, they raced to the fire house and completely wrecked the delivery wagon.

The incident led the merchants to buy a sprinkler, and the horses were used to pull this wagon. The members of the fire company and merchants made monthly payments for the sprinkler. An excursion helped raise funds for a water tower.

Fire struck again and again. A conflagration on April 1, 1898, destroyed the Opera House building, which also contained a number of offices. The *Enterprise* had its location there and, because of the loss of equipment, was forced to suspend publication for several weeks. New Iberia had a destructive fire in October, 1899. This one, the most damaging ever experienced in the town, spread rapidly. It was beyond control before the fire department could start operations. (Jeanerette and St. Martinville sent their fire engines to help.) An entire square bounded by Main, St. Peter, Iberia, and Julia Streets was destroyed, as well as residences and buildings on the opposite side of these streets. The total loss was estimated at $250,000. The property was insured for about $125,000.

Reconstruction and plans for better protection began promptly. Two weeks later three brick buildings were started. In general, better buildings replaced the old. The State Bank was the first to resume business in the burned district, starting operations in their rebuilt quarters December 16, 1899.

The same month that this fire occurred, a new fire company was organized to take the place of an older one. There were thirty-six charter members in this group. Since, there has been a continual growth of New Iberia's fire department, and the city now has five fire stations.

For fifteen years press comments, editorials, and meetings pointed out the need of a public water supply; eventually at the turn of the century, New Iberia acquired waterworks. In this respect New Iberia was behind Jeanerette, which had acquired waterworks in 1895. It was reported, in 1899, that New Iberia was the only town in Louisiana with a population of 5,000 or more without a waterworks system.

A test of the waterworks plant was made in March, 1901. A stream of water from a fifty-foot section of hose shot easily over the tower of the City Hall, under a pressure of one hundred pounds.

In May, 1901, this new water system was used to put out a fire for the first time.

A move was made, in 1899, to buy from Sylvio Broussard the electric light and power plant, which was the source of water and lights for the town and which was, many people thought, an unsatisfactory system.

Finally, in the autumn of 1900, there was a favorable election for the authorization of a $40,000 bond issue, supported by a three-mill tax for the erection of a waterworks and electric light plant for New Iberia.

In 1885, New Iberia obtained electric lights. Records show a contract being awarded to N. Stansbury for $34.50 a month for street lights.[5] But in 1898, the town had been without street lights for six months, and another contract was made—this time with Sylvio Broussard, who was to provide the town with one hundred lights for $125.00 a month.

About the middle of April, 1901, the town was lighted for the first time by alternating circuits. By June, 1902, the electric light plant was no longer an expense to the taxpayers, as the earnings were exceeding the operating expenses.

At a later date it was believed that it would be better to have water and electricity furnished by a private company. In 1925, Gulf Public Service Company, Incorporated came to New Iberia for that purpose. The first merged, in 1946, with the Louisiana Public Utilities Company and kept its name. Again there was a merger, in 1951, with the Central Louisiana Electric Company. CLECO furnishes electricity, water, and gas to the parish. The city of New Iberia is furnished gas by the United Gas Corporation which began operations here September 10, 1931.

JEANERETTE

The town in the parish next in importance to New Iberia is Jeanerette. This area was probably first settled by Nicholas Provost, who emigrated to Louisiana in 1780. Although he may have received a grant of one square league, when Provost's succession was filed in St. Mary Parish, it was listed as having approximately 3,000 acres. Using present day landmarks, the land would extend on the east from the St. Mary Parish line to the west on the Experimental Farm line, and from Bayou Teche to the Forty Arpent Road. There was also a tract of land east of the bayou. The property owned by Provost is where Jeanerette is located. It is interesting to note that the grandson of Nicholas Edmond Provost became Jeanerette's first mayor.

---

[5]No records were found to show that the town had electric lights prior to 1885.

Another early inhabitant in the area near Jeanerette was John G. Richardson, who came here from Mississippi in October, 1829. He bought land for a sugar plantation; it was known as the Richardson Place and later as Hope Plantation.

John W. Jeanerette, for whom the village was named[6] according to Alexandre Barde in his book published in 1861, came to this district about 1830 and bought what is known as Pine Grove. He was a sugar planter, justice of the peace, and for about three years, from February 25, 1830, was the first postmaster between New Iberia and Charenton. In 1837 he moved to Alabama. The St. Martin Succession Records show that on July 9, 1848, John W. Jeanerette's widow wanted to have his estate settled, as the owner had recently died.

Records show a long list of postmasters following John W. Jeanerette. They were Charles Nettleton, William Smith, William H. Basset, William Smith, F. D. Richardson, Nicholas Provost, Adrien Viville, Clet Provost, Thomas J. McCarty, Ursin Provost, Jr., Paul Provost, William F. Hudson, Alex W. Edgar, James J. Lemon, Aristide Monnot, and Charles Judice, who was serving when Jeanerette was incorporated March 15, 1878. The next postmaster was an ex-slave, Mose Frazier, who held the position from May 29, 1882 to March 8, 1883.

When Richardson was postmaster, the Post Office was moved two miles south of its first location on Jeanerette's place, opposite Bayside and near a famous black live oak stump which stood there, up to 1900, as a gloomy sentinel. This landmark gave to the area the name Chicot Noir (black stump).

A petition was made to change the name of the Jeanerette Post Office in this area to Chicot Noir, and later, when the Post Office was moved a mile farther south with Provost as postmaster, an attempt was made to change the name to Provostville. In both instances the Post Master General refused the request. It is around this third location that the village of Jeanerette began to grow.

The building up of Jeanerette was partly due to the building of a saw-mill by Joseph S. Whitworth and his associates.

---

[6]No records have been found for Jean Erette for whom some say Jeanerette was named.

By 1860, there were in Jeanerette a hotel, a fine store, and about forty houses. In 1854 W. F. Hudson came from Franklin to establish a store. He was postmaster for a while. Hudson is, by some, called the Father of Jeanerette. He later started the Plantation Supply Store and Mercantile Business, which was sold to F. J. de Gravelle in 1892. Aristide L. Monnot, a native of Vaufrey, France established the first sugar manufacturing plant in this section on his plantation Vaufrey.

A blacksmith shop, which eventually grew into a foundry, was established by A. Moresi. Moresi also established the first brick yard in Jeanerette, and, in 1885, the first successful plant for manufacturing ice.

Jeanerette's first newspaper was founded by Dr. C. A. McGowen, who went there in 1879 as a dental surgeon. He opened a drug store and later a general mercantile business.

In 1870 Jeanerette was the center of an extensive agricultural district. It had five good stores, the best saw mill on the bayou, a gunsmith, a hotel, a coffeehouse, a good private school, two harness shops, butcher shops, a barber shop, and other minor establishments. In 1880 the population of Jeanerette was 698, and in 1890 it was 1,309. By April, 1897, an iron bridge across the Teche was completed at Jeanerette.

The Beaulieu and Monnin families were also some of the early settlers in Jeanerette. Among others who later added to the growth of the section were St. Paul Bourgeois, John Bussey, Paul N. Cyr, Jr., Lieutenant-Governor of Louisiana in 1931, the Moresi Brothers, H. B. Hewes, and Edward Jackson.

LOREAUVILLE

The village of Loreauville, primarily an agricultural center, was named in the 1840's for Ozaire Loreau from France. Mr. Loreau gave the property for the Catholic Church and for the cemetery.

Ozaire's brother, Joseph Loreau, also owned land in this area. The original settlers of this district were French; later some Acadians came to make Loreauville their home.

Some people say that Loreauville was known earlier as Picouville or Picotville, for a family by the name of Picou or Picot.

In 1899, the bridge across the Teche was completed. When

it was incorporated, April 23, 1910, Loreauville had a population of 291. Its first mayor was C. F. Berard.

Adrien Gonsoulin and his son-in-law, John D. Walet, were instrumental in the growth of the town. Gonsoulin constructed the area's first railroad so that his cane could be transported from his plantation to his sugar mill. Gonsoulin owned a saw mill and a store and gave employment to many people. John D. Walet had a store, a cotton gin, and much property in the section. Walet was a member of the school board and was influential in the life of the community.

Before the war between the states Dr. Angus Steven Shaw settled in the Loreauville area. The life of his family had some influence on the community. On one occasion his sons built the first bicycle in Loreauville of the type having one very large wheel and one small wheel. The first ride taken by Guy Shaw landed him in the bayou. This bicycle did not prove satisfactory so a more conventional bicycle was constructed.

When the boys were young, about in 1880, they imported Italian bees, the first in this section. The profits from this apiary, saved in gold, were used to educate first J. W. K. Shaw, then Guy A. Shaw for the medical profession. Bee culture was financially more profitable than medicine. Queens of the "Shawline" of bees were shipped to countries the world over. Dr. Guy Shaw continued to receive orders and inquiries about bees for more than twenty years after he stopped propagating bees for shipment. When a sister moved to California she took some of the bees along. Dr. Shaw kept about thirty hives until the time of his death in 1941.

Another first in Loreauville was the purchase of an automobile by Dr. Guy Shaw about 1902. Before the automobile could be driven from the railroad station the directions for running the car had to be studied. Riding ahead of the new automobile was a friend who cleared the way for the safety of any who might be around.

Many other people contributed to the growth of Loreauville, among whom were the Bonin, Dugas, Breaux, Judice, Ransonnet, Oubre, LeBlanc, Vaughan, Berard, and Prince families. Some of the present industries adding to the prosperity of the area are oil, lumber, boat building, and agriculture.

OTHER SETTLEMENTS

There are a number of other small settlements in the parish; Avery Island is one. The Attakapas Indians were afraid of the island and could not be induced to go to the place because of the legend of a great catastrophe occurring there. Yet relics of stone implements and a woven basket exactly like the ones made by the Attakapas Indians have been found at a depth of sixteen feet. It is said that along with these relics have been found pieces of matting made of southern cane (one of them nearly two feet square), and pottery with images of the mastadon. Bones of the animals have been found in strata eight to ten feet above those of man.

One of the earliest land grants on the island was made to Elizabeth Hayes by the Spanish government. She was living there about 1790.

About the time that John Craig Marsh bought land on both banks of the Teche, about 1828, he also bought land on Avery Island or what was then Petite Anse Island. He established a sugar plantation with all that was necessary to make a success of the business.

The St. Martin Parish records show that Margaret H. Marsh, the wife of A. B. Henshaw, sold one-third of Petite Anse Island plantation to Daniel D. Avery on April 19, 1854. Avery was a resident of Baton Rouge. For a while Avery Island was known as Marsh Island.

The McIlhenny family is another of the Avery Island families. Edward Avery McIlhenny did much to make the island one of the beauty spots of the world. Bird City has tens of thousands of snowy egrets and as many other birds. Jungle Gardens has about ten thousand camellia plants of about five hundred varieties and about thirty thousand azaleas of over a hundred forms. There are plants imported from many foreign countries. One of these imported plants is a Wasi orange tree, given as a reward to McIlhenny for having saved the lives of three influential Japanese from a sinking vessel. At that time there were only two other orange trees like it, both of them in the imperial gardens of Tokyo.

Avery Island has developed into a prosperous industrial cen-

Iberia Parish Court House constructed in 1884. The Iberia Steam Fire Co. No. 1 is shown with the foreman, Laurent Bazus, and the sponsor, Josephine Emmer, June 16, 1911.

Joseph Jefferson Home, Jefferson Island, La.

A view of Mt. Carmel Convent showing the part that was the Frederick Duperier Home, said to be the first house built on the east side of Bayou Teche in New Iberia.

City Hall, Delcambre, Louisiana.

Shrimp Boat at Delcambre.

ter for salt, oil, and tabasco pepper and has a population of more than 800.

Jefferson Island was a Spanish grant made to Prevost and Carline. Joseph Carline was in the Attakapas District as early as 1774. The tract, ceded by Miro contained 200 acres with an elevation of about ninety feet above sea level. The plantation passed into the ownership of a Scotchman by the name of Randolph, who planted many fruit and pecan trees. The place, called at first Cote Carlin, became Orange Island. There were about 6,000 orange trees, 2,000 pecan trees, many of the better kind of cherry trees, some fig, peach, lemon, and quince trees. Randolph was said to be a brother-in-law of the pirate Jean Laffite.

The island was sold, in 1825, by Randolph to F. J. Miller. The place was then known as Miller's Island. At a later date the property was acquired by Faustin Dupuy from whom Joseph Jefferson bought the land in 1870.

Jefferson, who is renowned for his roles in "Rip Van Winkle" and "The Rivals," purchased more land and surrounded his estate by a thick hedge of cherokee roses about seven miles in circumference. Another cherokee rose hedge about three miles in circumference was planted around the home which he had built about 1886. This home constructed with native cypress has been preserved in its original state.

Some of Laffite's treasure was said to have been buried on Jefferson Island. In 1923, Daynite, called by some a voodoo man, while digging a culvert unearthed three pots containing Spanish, Mexican, and American coins. Many other people have dug in vain around the lake and under trees in this small community.

Still another place settled as a plantation was Weeks Island, or Grand Cote as it was named then. In 1792, a grant of 800 arpents was made by Carondelet to Don William Weeks, and 400 arpents to Richard Bell. Josua Garret and Gideon Hopkins also received grants. At the time Weeks was the only one who built cabins and made fields on his grant. But when the cabins and fields were abandoned, Louis de Blanc claimed the entire island, which was given to him while a law suit was pending. De Blanc lost the suit, and the land went back to the original grantees.

In 1897, the Weeks and Myles corporation was formed for the purpose of mining salt. Today the village of Weeks is company owned, and the island is a center for salt and oil industry.

Delcambre is a small town located in Vermilion Parish as well as in Iberia Parish. It received its name from early settlers who came from Brest, France, and who were here under Spanish rule. One of the settlers in the area, here at least in the early 1800's, was Charles Delcambre. It was Desire Delcambre who donated the land on which stands the Catholic Church and it is believed that the town was named after him. Some Acadians also settled there, and today there are still a few direct descendants of these Acadians.

Delcambre was incorporated as a village on November 27, 1907, under the provisions of the Louisiana Legislative Act 136 of 1898. It was reclassified as the Town of Delcambre by Governor's proclamation on June 3, 1946.

The village at first had three councilmen: Desire Delcambre, Homer Landry, and A. T. Delcambre. Alcee Dronet was marshall, Theodore Trahan was treasurer, and A. T. Delcambre was clerk and secretary. The first mayor was Pierre Pelloat.

A few dates to be remembered in the history of Delcambre are: October, 1908, application was made for depot facilities; 1910, a bank was built; December, 1911, a water system for the village was installed; 1938, the City Hall and a new water-works plant were constructed.

Probably Dr. Alfred Duperier first cared for the sick in the Delcambre area. Dr. Tuson served the community and was followed by Dr. Adolph Landry. Dr. Landry was the first Delcambre citizen to own a car. This car, a Lindsley, acquired about 1910, reesembled a buggy. It had lanterns on either side, as did the carriages of the day, and extra gas was always carried in a tank in the car.

Today Delcambre is especially known as a center of the shrimping industry. An ice house there makes do-nut ice, which is produced every fifteen minutes.

Other small places in the parish, which were little more than shipping stations with a post office and a store or two were Cade, Olivier, Burke, Belle Place, Derouen, Morbihan, and Patoutville. The last was a center of trade for people of Isle

Piquant and Cypremort prairies, and in 1888 had a public school and a church.

During the early period the progress of the towns and villages was slow but steady. All the settlements depended on the surrounding agricultural districts. The places more favorably located for transportation became the larger commercial centers.

CHAPTER V

COMMERCE AND INDUSTRY

The parish of Iberia owes its growth and prosperity to its location which is favorable for transportation and communication, and the development and use of natural resources in industry. The parish grew steadily from a population of 9,042 in 1870 to 16,676 in 1880; 20,997 in 1890; and 29,015 in 1900.

The first transportation to this district was by Bayou Teche. One of the boats registered in 1817 belonged to Francois Maingonnat, who was also its master. This 31 31/95-ton keel-boat, *Eliza*, was built in Tennessee to be used here on the Teche. Other boats of this same period owned by Iberians were the *Buck, Plough Boy, Attakapas, Teche*, and the *Rachel*. Some of the steamboats used from 1850 to 1854 were the *Delia*, captained by Ed Castillio; the *Ross* of Captain William Greig; and the *Ceres* of Captain Laborth. These boats ran from New Orleans by way of Plaquemine Bayou to St. Martinville. The trip was made in twenty-four hours. The steamer *Minnie Avery* was one of the most popular in the 1870's. Another steamer, which made regular trips to New Iberia was the *Peerless*. Another, the *Iberia*, was noted for being behind time because of heavy freights. The Pharr line of steamers was so overworked carrying sugar, molasses, and other freight that the ships frequently reached Morgan City late from New Iberia, but they still managed to make mail connections both ways.

To remove obstructions such as wrecked boats and stumps from Bayou Teche, the Federal Government, in 1851, appropriated $17,000. A naval lieutenant was sent out by the government to inspect the work being done. Later two canals were dug—the Attakapas Canal, which led from Petite Anse prairie to Vermilion Bay, and the Grand Cote Canal, from Isle Piquant prairie to Grand Cote Bay. These canals linked the Teche valley with the Lafourche and Mississippi.

In 1905 the Commercial Canal was begun. The following year

the Bayou Carlin Canal was completed. In 1911 the Intracoastal Canal was cut across the lower part of Iberia Parish. This canal is accessible to New Iberia.

About the middle of the 1880's a coincidence occurred in the destruction of two boats belonging to the same owner, Captain Bell. At exactly the same spot at the foot of Camelia Street in New Iberia, the boats were destroyed. The *Key West*, on its regular bi-weekly trip, hit a cypress stump covered by the high water; the hull was ripped open, and the boat sank. The other boat, the *Chambers*, came with a large steam pump, and with the help of divers succeeded in bringing up the *Key West*, which was adequately repaired to make the trip to New Orleans, where it was fully restored. Two weeks later, when the *Chambers* was returning from St. Martinville, it caught fire at the bend in Bayou Teche and sank at the Cypress stump.

The spring of 1871 saw another new 120-foot wharf built in New Iberia. A short time later another warehouse was erected. Advances in shipping continued in the parish.

When the railroad was constructed, a new means of transportation was added in the parish.

By May, 1857, a railroad at Berwick Bay could be reached by steamboat from any point on Bayou Teche. A roadway for a railroad was begun at New Iberia, in 1858, westward to Vermilionville. It was reported, in January, 1861, that a roadway from Berwick Bay to New Iberia would be completed in about two months, except for a stretch of one and one-half miles of swamp land. At the same time the roadway from New Iberia to Vermilionville was reaching completion. By 1862 this whole roadway of sixty-three miles, with the exception of the swamp area, was ready for track-laying. The blockade during the Civil War, however, stopped the delivery of rails. Then in 1872, ten years later, a little work was done to prepare again this roadway for track-laying. This work was done by the New Orleans, Mobile, and Texas Railroad, the new title for the Morgan Louisiana and Texas Railroad. In August of the same year the work was again abandoned.

Finally, in 1879, the track was laid in Iberia Parish. The railroad passed through the east side of the parish, going up northwest to Vermilionville. Later a branch was built from

New Iberia to the Avery salt mine. In the 1890's another branch was extended to Abbeville. At the close of the century, the old passenger station was moved back and used as a freight station, and a new passenger station was erected east of the tracks. The station was opened for service on January 3, 1901. Extra tracks and facilities were being added to keep up with the growth and business of the city. The Missouri Pacific Lines began to operate in New Iberia in 1910.

The roads of the parish were always a problem and mention of this is found scattered throughout the Police Jury minutes. The State Legislature required the parishes to have a special road tax; therefore, a tax of one-fourth of one per cent of all the real and personal property within the limits of the parish of Iberia was levied, according to the assessed value in the tax rolls. To supervise and direct all road work done within their district, two syndics, or commissioners, were appointed. They were to receive five dollars for each work day and one dollar for each written report made to the Police Jury. The road overseers were entitled to ten per cent of all fines collected from those landowners who failed to build bridges over drainage ditches.

In 1871 the construction of nine roads was authorized. These roads were to form a good network over the parish, connecting settlements in which there was no direct land passage. One of the roads planned was from New Iberia to Lafayette Parish. In 1873 a committee was appointed to examine the possibility of a road to the line of Lafayette Parish and report the results of the examination. Then, in 1876, a committee was appointed to secure the right of way from the people of the different parishes through which the road would pass. Such projects were long in being carried out.

In order to expedite road construction, in 1877, the Police Jury passed a resolution to the effect that all male residents of the parish would have to work, on the parish roads, twelve days in the year. They would be given ten days written notice and would have to pay one dollar a day for failure to do the work. Making the inhabitants responsible for road work appears to be customary. Violations were punishable by a thirty dollar fine or imprisonment. One was allowed to pay another person to do his work. Two months later this resolution was amended to require only four days of work.

Editors of newspapers were constantly urging road improvements. To strengthen their argument, they cited experiences caused by the bad roads. The *Louisiana Sugar Bowl* tells of a man who left New Iberia for St. Martinville. About five miles out, his horse and buggy became stuck in the mud; he had to return home. The papers reminded their readers that the towns were losing trade because, in bad weather, the roads were impassable for loaded wagons. Many of the roads were described as being "in disgraceful condition." Another newspaper story found in a *Daily Iberian* in 1894 tells of Edmond Laperouse, who went to the editor's office to complain of the bad condition of the roads and the dilapidated conditions of two bridges located outside the city limits. Mr. Laperouse said that, since the police jurors were his friends, he wanted to warn them of this condition, lest they be hurt or killed. Discontent over roads had reached that pitch.

For many years before 1897 road improvement was attempted. Many loads of brick bats were put on Main Street in New Iberia. In 1897 between seven and ten thousand barrels of oyster shells were used to improve the street. In 1899 several car loads of shells were used for the portion of Main Street already shelled and to continue shelling the street to the corner of Prairie Avenue. The City Council decided, in 1902, to put oyster shells on all the town streets between the railroad and the bayou.

The streets were not always kept in good condition, however, as one story tells of a chicken bogging in the mud while crossing the street in front of the Frederick Hotel. This happened as late as 1914.

In 1912, in Iberia Parish, a "model road" was made as an experiment by Governor J. Y. Sanders. The experimental road was from the Lietmeyer Woods to the eastern extremity of Jeanerette. It was the first bitulithic compound road in the state. In winter the road was crusty and hard and in summer, so soft that the cane carts made ruts in the composition. Of course this type of road was not successful, and after a while it was ploughed up and gravel put down.

The New Iberia records show that in 1919 Main Street was

paved from the Weeks Street to the North Street intersections. The portion between Weeks Street and Railroad Avenue was laid with bricks. In 1925-1926 East Main was paved from Weeks Street to Louis Avenue. At this time other streets, including Duperier Avenue, were paved.

At the beginning of 1900 concrete sidewalks were replacing brick and board walks on Main Street and, later, all over town. The sidewalks were put down "here and there," as the owner of the property saw fit. The 1905 records show that four miles of sidewalks, five and one-half feet wide, were being planned at a cost of $40,000.00.

From 1900 to 1906 at least three people were granted franchises to construct a street railway, but each franchise was forfeited. Finally, about 1913, the Interurban Trolley Company, headed by F. M. Crosby, provided transportation from North Street in New Iberia to the eastern end of Jeanerette at the St. Mary Parish boundary line. Four trips daily were made between New Iberia and Jeanerette. This service continued until about 1917.

The earliest mail or postal route records available show that in January, 1814, a contract was let to Joseph Aborn for service on a route from "Blanchards, by La Fourche, Donalds Town, Assumption, mouth of Teche River, Berwick Bay, Cypress Swamp, New Town, Attakapas Court House, to Opelousas Court House." The schedule provided that the mails should leave Blanchards at noon on Sundays, arrive at Opelousas Court House by 6 P. M. the following Wednesdays, leave Opelousas Court House at 6 A. M. Thursdays, and arrive at Blanchards by 10 A. M. the following Sundays. The manner of transportation is not indicated.

In 1871, the mail from New Iberia to Neblett's Bluff, Texas, went by stage on Tuesdays, Thursdays, and Saturdays. The mail came by boat from Berwick Bay, and then it was sent by stage coach from New Iberia to Texas. An order from the Post Office Department in 1899 said that all mail for St. Martinville, like that of other post offices in the immediate vicinity, was to be delivered to New Iberia and distributed from that point.

In the town paper in the late 1800's, occasionally there appears a list of the names of persons having, at the post office, letters which had not been claimed.

New Iberia first had a post office of its own in 1814. Shortly before April 1, 1809, Nathan Morse was appointed Postmaster of "Attakapas or St. Martinville, or New Iberia." Later the name was changed to St. Martinville, New Iberia's first postmaster was James Miller. Succeeding postmasters were Joseph Aborn, Josiah French, Clarkson Edgar,[1] Achille Berard,[2] John Taylor, Abner D. Miner, John De Valcourt,[3] Josiah French, John De Valcourt, Luther M. Sugg, Robert I. Epperson, Abner D. Miner, Wm. G. Daunt, Pierre L. Renoudet, I. R. Esnard, Wm. A. Riggs, Samuel Wakefield (Negro), Charles Decuir (Negro), Carmelite C. Guilfoux, Robert Brantley, Casimir Burkhart, Alexander Cestia, Thos. R. Morse, Alphonse Davis (acting), Sylvio Broussard, B. P. LeMoine (acting), and Van Harry.

Until 1903, the New Iberia Post Office was a small cubby hole, moved from pillar to post, and was inadequate except for the short time it was located in the Opera House.

In 1900 Congress appropriated $60,000 for a post office in New Iberia. The lot on the south corner of Weeks and Main Streets was sold by Levy and Davis, agents for the owners, Pointis and Delcambre. The post office was constructed by the Messrs. Bradt and Company of Atlanta. On October 10, 1903, the Postmaster T. R. Morse, moved in.

In 1901, in preparation for free mail delivery, the New Iberia City Council made plans to have all street signs and numbers on buildings in readiness. There were to be three letter carriers, one substitute carrier, and eighteen street letter boxes. This mail delivery began about November 1, 1903.

Other means of communication had also been provided. About the time of the Civil War, a telegraph line had been built from Algiers to New Iberia, a distance of 125 miles. The Baltimore and Ohio Telegraph line also served New Iberia. In 1885, E. F. Millard was in charge of the office. In June, 1898, the Postal

---

[1]The name of the post office was changed to Nova Iberia.
[2]The settlement was again called New Iberia.
[3]The town was incorporated when John De Valcourt served as postmaster.

Telegraph Company opened an office in New Iberia. Shortly thereafter Western Union located in New Iberia.

The next means of communication to serve New Iberia was the telephone. The files of the Southern Bell Telephone and Telegraph Company show that the New Iberia Exchange was established in 1893 by Great Southern Telephone Company, with seventeen subscribers. The Exchange was acquired, in 1898, by the Cumberland Telephone and Telegraph Company, which also established the Jeanerette Exchange the same year with ten subscribers. The New Iberia Telephone Exchange was granted a charter in September, 1895. The People's Independent Telephone Company competed with the Cumberland Telephone and Telegraph Company, in New Iberia for several years prior to its acquisition by the Cumberland in 1906. In April of that same year the Southern Bell Telephone and Telegraph Company purchased, on the market, enough Cumberland stock to control the company. All remaining Cumberland stock was acquired by Southern Bell in 1926.

The system was converted to common battery January 24, 1931, and to the dial system February 7, 1953. The Jeanerette Exchange converted from magneto to dial on October 1, 1949.

In the fall of 1871 New Iberia was described as a thriving commercial district. Since the formation of the parish, seventy-five new stores and places of business had been establshed. There were agents for the many makes of sewing machines, and agents for life and fire insurance companies. In 1878, a new ice factory was opened, which had a capacity to manufacture five tons of ice daily. There was a cistern factory which made cypress cisterns and tanks. Another industry was the manufacture of Tabasco pepper sauce, which Edmund McIlhenny developed from pepper seeds brought to him in 1852 from southern Mexico by his friend Gleason. The combination oil mill and soap factory, began in 1878 by Judge Gates, was, ten years later, said to be the most extensive manufacturing enterprise in New Iberia. Among the various other businesses were several brickyards.

At this time many sugar mills were found scattered throughout the parish. One of the oldest was the Enterprise Sugar Factory, which was founded by Isadore Patout in the 1830's. At first the mill, with a capacity of six hundred tons, was horsepowered. The sugar mill burned in the spring of 1959 and was rebuilt for the fall grinding. It is now incorporated as M. A. Patout and Son, Limited. The Central Sugar Manufactory of Messrs. Martin and Childs was expected to make two million pounds of sugar before stopping in February, 1888. Bagasse had been used in the furnace and had proved very satisfactory.

In January, 1896, the people of Iberia Parish were asking for its first refinery. Within an hour, signatures were collected with endorsements for $2,000. By July the work on the refinery was in full swing. It was to have a capacity of twelve thousand tons a day. This Segura Mill produced raw sugar until it was destroyed by fire on August 11, 1912.

Today Iberia Parish has five sugar mills. Just outside the New Iberia city limits is the Iberia Sugar Cooperative, which was established in 1937.

Lumbering was the most important single industry of New Iberia in 1885. One of the earliest saw mills, located on Camelia Street, was owned by Frederick Mestayer. In 1871, the demand for lumber could not be supplied by three mills in New Iberia, and a planing mill was established. This mill had all the machinery necessary for first class sash, door, and blind work. The new saw mill of Messrs. Gall and Pharr was kept running constantly. The old mill owned by these men was not kept running all the time. The large mill of the P. L. Renoudet Cypress Company, on Big Jim Lane, supplied, in 1899, the heavy cypress timbers that were used for a bridge across the Teche at St. John Plantation in St. Martin Parish. The timber land of the parish furnished cypress, oak, ash, magnolia, sweet gum, hackberry, and other varieties.

The Iberia Cypress Company on Big Jim Lane had, besides the saw mill, a large boarding house, and a store that was patronized by many New Iberia families. The store furnished a delivery service. The little settlement had telephones, electric lights, and a water-works plant.

Salt has, for years, been an important mineral in Iberia Parish. Known to the early Indians, the salt springs of Petite Anse were rediscovered in 1791. Solid salt was discovered in 1862, when a business of "forty baskets a day" was promoted. After the war several companies leased the mines. In 1899 the

International Salt Company took over. A five-hundred-foot shaft was sunk, and has been used continuously ever since.

The discovery of salt beds on Cote Carlin, or Jefferson Island, in March, 1895, led to the exploration of the entire region. Salt was not immediately mined at Jefferson Island, as Joe Jefferson did not want to spoil the beauty of the place. In 1901, boring on Jefferson Island by Captain A. F. Lucas of Spindle-Top oil fame showed that there was rock salt starting at three hundred feet and extending to at least two thousand one hundred feet. However, operations were suspended because development was so difficult and expensive. The island was purchased in 1917 by a group of Kentucky business men for a hunting preserve. They operated a rice and sugar plantation and raised Brahma and Black Angus cattle. The salt mining business began in 1920 by sinking the largest round shaft in the world, one hundred feet in circumference. The Diamond Crystal Salt Company of St. Clair, Michigan acquired the plant and mine in 1957.

On Grand Cote, or Weeks Island, development of the salt industry began before the turn of the century, but the first carload of salt was not sold until January, 1901. This shipment was made to the wholesale house of Jules Dreyfus in New Iberia.

Iberia Parish could boast of still another gift from nature— the fish found in coastal and inland waters. Lake Tasse or Spanish Lake, and Lake Peigner (so called because of its fanciful resemblance to a wool-comber,) or Lake Simonette, were filled with fish of every kind found in the region. Some of the trout were said to have been two and a half feet long.

The shrimping industry with its center at Delcambre has become an important industry of the parish. The Delcambre Canal, which leads to Vermilion Bay and the shrimping waters, was first dredged, in 1906, by Louis Angers and has become the key to the prosperity of Delcambre.

Trapping for furs is another source of income for the inhabitants. Muskrats, mink, otter, nutria, and other fur bearing animals are caught during the season, which lasts approximately three months. The trappers leave home to live in small camps or houseboats in the coastal marshes, where all the family are kept busy with the work of looking after the traps, cleaning and curing the furs, and other regular work around the camp.

The Main Street Central Market, located where the City Hall now stands, opened in New Iberia, March 1, 1899. It was built by the town at a cost of $12,809.28. The Board of Trustees passed an ordinance, for the town limits, which allowed the selling, of meat or fish of any kind, poultry, game, vegetables, etc., only in the new market. (Potatoes, onions, cabbage, beans, and peas could be sold at grocery stores.) There were also regulations for leasing and renting stalls, sanitary rules, condition of products sold, and safety and order in the market. In time the ordinance regulating the sale of produce was changed. About 1927 the market was closed; and in 1933 the building was torn down to make way for the new City Hall.

The economic status of Iberia Parish did not keep pace with its population growth. Even though business prospered, the condition of the parish treasury was poor in 1871. As can be seen in the Police Jury proceedings a new evaluation of property was decided upon in order to equalize assessments and taxes. The minutes show that it was not thought advisable, because of agricultural failures, to add a tax for the construction of a railroad from Berwick Bay to Washington, Louisiana. In 1873, to reduce the taxation, which was thought to be keeping away farmers who might come to this area, a special road tax of four mills was repealed, and the office of Road Overseer abolished. Conditions were still bad in 1874. Because of the extreme poverty of the people and the difficulty they felt in paying even the smallest amount of taxes, the Jury passed a resolution that the greatest economy possible should be practiced. There was owed to the parish, at this time, the sum of $19,268.47. This sum represented delinquent taxes and had been accumulating since the formation of the parish.

Other items give a view of economic conditions, such as the appropriation, in 1877, of forty cents a day for the maintenance of prisoners. The *Iberia Progress* in 1877, in speaking of the general state of affairs, said that game was in abundance, eggs plentiful, groceries inactive, politics dull. Everything was plentiful, and everyone happy; yet taxpayers could not see the "joint de retrenchment." There were numerous taxes and licenses. The tax on all non-residents of the parish crossing any of the public bridges or ferries was five cents for every footman and up to twenty-five cents for a four-wheel vehicle. The highest parish license for 1878 was one of $1,000 for proprietors of gambling houses. Then, as always, taxes were a cause for complaint. In 1885 and in 1902 articles in the local papers showed that financial conditions were bad.

Beginning in 1893 and until 1903, there appear in the local papers many articles concerning the single tax—a tax on land values irrespective of improvements. The idea, expounded by Henry George, was to abolish all other taxes, raise the tax on land to meet the necessary expenses for the local, state, and national governments, and divide the revenue accordingly. Poverty and its effects were supposed to disappear under this system. The interest in this system was not only national but world-wide. In time, interest in the subject was lost.

The first foundry and machine shop was established by Stott and Lutzenberger in 1870. At that time all who raised sugar cane also ground the cane, and the work of keeping numerous mills in order and of erecting new mills gave abundant and profitable work to the foundry. Much of the work of the foundry was also with boats. The last casting by Stott and Lutzenberger was made in 1953. That early foundry is now the New Iberia Foundry and Supply Company.

Plans were made as far back as 1871 for a bank in New Iberia, but it was not until 1887 that the New Iberia National Bank was established. The next bank in the town was the People's National Bank, organized in 1891. The State Bank of New Iberia opened for business in September, 1897, after the vault was completed but before all the fixtures were installed.

In the late 1880's the merchants, manufacturers, and business men of New Iberia belonged to the Mechanics and Traders Exchange. This organization was a kind of board of trade. It had officers, a board of directors, and rooms in which could be found on file all the leading newspapers of the country.

A meeting to organize a Board of Trade was held at the suggestion of S. P. Watts, who wrote a series of editorials on the need of such a civic body. Following Watt's suggestion, local business and professional leaders organized, in February, 1893, a Board of Trade. Newspaper files suggest that the Board of Trade and similar organizations were intermittently active and inactive, depending on the interest of the members. The Chamber of Commerce is considered an outgrowth of the Board of Trade. In 1914, A. C. Bernard came here to organize the New Iberia Chamber of Commerce. Mr. Bernard was the first secretary. About six years later he was presented with the first and only honorary life membership for his services to the organization.

The New Iberia Rice Milling Company began to operate the first rice mill in New Iberia in 1899 and was located near the bayou banks on the west end of town. In 1902, this company merged with the Attakapas Ginning Company and the Iberia Oil and Soap Works to form the New Iberia Milling and Development Co. In the 1880's New Iberia had four cotton gins.

At the beginning of the present century, the people of Iberia Parish became very interested in discovering oil. This "oil fever" was evident in the formation of drilling companies, in which many citizens made investments, and in drilling by private individuals on their own property. Digging for oil became the talk of the town. However, it was not until 1917 that the "oil fever" changed to effective oil development. By 1950 there were eight producing oil fields. Today the oil industry is one of the leading industries in Iberia Parish.

H. H. Caldwell, the general organizer of the American Federation of Labor, was in New Iberia in May, 1901, to organize a branch of the Federation. The second day that Caldwell was here, the men at George Simon's Machine Shop went on strike for a nine-hour day. (At this time a ten-hour day was usual.) In 1903, a column informing the public of labor's view on questions of the times was run in the *Weekly Iberian*, a local newspaper. In 1903 organized labor celebrated Labor Day with street parades, speeches, a baseball game, and a dance.[4]

The 1840's saw New Iberia become the center of trade for sixty miles in all directions. During the low stage of water, large gulf steamers were not able to go above New Iberia. Therefore, the cargoes for all points south and west on the Vermilion and Calcasieu, were landed at New Iberia.

The Port of New Iberia, which is located about four miles

---

[4]The parade for the colored people was held in the morning and for the white in the afternoon.

south of New Iberia, has added to the prosperity of the community. The Commercial Canal, which originated as a drainage canal, joins with the Intracoastal Canal about seven miles to the south of the port. The first port commission, after the channel was dug and completed, was appointed in 1948.

Work on the Naval Auxiliary Air Station in Iberia Parish began in 1957. In 1959, many of the personnel were already located at the base which was in full operation in 1960. The Navy base is dedicated to training anti-submarine pilots.

Business and industry in Iberia Parish are progressing steadily. New Iberia is showing this growth by developing several shopping centers away from the main district of the city Under consideration at this writing are plans for a Civic Center destined to include a new post office and city hall. The site of this proposed Civic Center is to be the land on which the old St. Peter's College now stands.

The Monnot home, one of the early houses of Jeanerette, now belonging to the Moresi family.

Above—Street Car on Main Street, Jeanerette. Below—President Theodore Roosevelt at Jeanerette during his Bull Moose campaign tour, 1912.

St. Joseph Catholic Church at Loreauville, La.

The Oubre House, Loreauville.

CHAPTER VI

SOCIAL AND CULTURAL LIFE

The culture of the people of Iberia Parish can best be understood by knowing the things which were accomplished along these lines because of the interest of the citizens.

As far back as 1848 New Iberia had a public school. The growth of the public schools in the parish was slow, as it was thought that public schools were for the poor; and all who could afford to do so went to private schools. By 1871, however, the parish had eleven public schools. The president of the school board gave these figures for two of the schools: St. Paul School had 145 pupils, with an average attendance for February of 98; the Webster School had 77 pupils, with an average attendance of 47 in February.

The financial condition of schools during the 1870's was in an unsettled condition. In the summer of 1871 the Marsh School for colored boys and girls of Fausse Pointe was kept open throughout the entire vacation through contributions of the parents of the children. The following January the public schools of the parish was closed from want of funds and were not expected to reopen until March. Two private schools taught by public school teachers had opened during the enforced vacation. The school funds had to be used to rent schoolhouses when funds should have been raised for more suitable buildings. To help the situation, in April, 1872, a special school tax of one mill was levied on all taxable property; in 1874 the school tax was one and a half mills.

The Iberia High School, the first in New Iberia, was opened October 10, 1887, in what had been the Julia Street School, a one-room building. To defray the cost of making the Julia Street School a high school, the inhabitants of the area raised money by subscription. The first graduation for the New Iberia High School was held June 28, 1889. Because of the growth and crowded condition of this school a new building was constructed; and the Central High School opened its doors for its first session November 11, 1896. Outside of New Orleans it was the only brick school in the state. There were two floors above the seven-foot basement. It was considered a model school, with its slate blackboards and completely modern equipment. This school, paid for solely by the subscriptions raised in the community, was evidence of the cultural interest of Iberians. One of the leading figures in the establishment of the high school was William R. Burke, who might well be called "the father of public education in Iberia Parish." Later, another high school was constructed to meet the needs of the growing enrollment. The first session there began in the fall of 1922. Numerous schools have been built or enlarged to keep up with the needs of the parish.

In January, 1892, a group to form a High School Library Association met, and the following month the High School Library Association was incorporated. At the time it was the only incorporated school library outside of New Orleans and the only public school library. Good reference books and several hundred good classics were acquired through the generosity of the people of the community. Monthly programs consisting of speeches, recitations, debates, and other forms of entertainment were sponsored in order to obtain the funds necessary for the library. When the Central High School came into use, the library was moved there. W. M. Howe, the principal of the Iberia High School, did much to found the library, and his efforts were appreciated by the public.

Although the schools in the rural districts were not as advanced as in New Iberia, improvements were gradually being made. The new school building, which was nearing completion in Loreauville, was sufficiently advanced to accommodate a Christmas party in 1899. The Jeanerette High School was ready for use January 1, 1900.

Regular monthly meetings, or institutes which lasted all day, were held; all teachers, white and colored, were expected to attend. Others interested in popular education also attended the meetings. Programs for these meetings were varied, interesting, and beneficial. As an example, one of the programs included talks on primary history and advanced history, temperament of the child, keeping pupils after school and during intermissions, educational standards, and the use of stories. Practical illustrations of how to develop action in teaching the common branches of study, how to teach definitions, and how to plan a week's work for the different subjects in the different grades were illustrated.

The commencements and school entertainments always seemed to be of great interest to the general public. As an example, for the 1894 graduation, although the weather was threatening, the Opera House, where the exercises were held, had every seat taken upstairs and down, and all available space jammed. This was the usual kind of attendance.

Although, until 1870, there were good private English and French schools, none was permanent until the Sisters of Mt. Carmel opened a school October 19, 1870. Here instruction was given in the various branches of the French and English languages, morals, politeness, and family welfare. Originally the school was located near the Catholic Church, and in 1872 the present site was purchased from Frederick Duperier. The old Duperier home still forms a part of the Convent.

Among the many other private schools was the Attakapas Commercial and Industrial School, which opened Monday, January 8, 1872, under the supervision of members of the Congregation of the Holy Cross. Over forty boys entered this school the first month. A trade education and commercial training could be obtained there. Soon an addition was made to the school at a cost of $1,900. There were four teachers to guide the sixty pupils, of whom eight or ten were from New Orleans.

An announcement of the opening of a convent for colored girls was made by Father Beaubien in November, 1872; a promise to establish a school for colored boys was also made. This school for girls was located where St. Peter's Rectory stands on the corner of St. Peter and Iberia Streets and was the first location for the Mt. Carmel sisters.

One of the renowned private schools of the district was the Fasnacht Institute, which was organized in 1891. The school provided primary instruction and continued on through high school training. The high school department was accredited, and the graduates were admitted to schools of higher learning.

After 1867 New Iberia had a private school for the colored, the Howe Institute, which was endowed by Northern philanthropy. The work being done there was of great benefit to the colored population.

The Howe Institute building, which was located on the site of the present Iberia Parish Courthouse, was first a home built by Dr. Leonard Smith and later, in 1862, became a school for white young ladies. In 1867, because of yellow fever in the area, two of the five teachers left for California; another married. With only two teachers remaining, the girls' school was forced to close.

Another of the private schools in New Iberia was a boys' school which held classes, beginning in 1903, at St. Berchman's Hall, under the supervision of the Mt. Carmel sisters. An adjoining home, presently Dauterive Hospital, was purchased for the increased enrollment. With the opening of St. Peter's College, a school for boys, in September, 1918, the school was discontinued. St. Peter's College was first located on the site of the old Henshaw home on Main Street. It has become Catholic High, situated on Admiral Doyle Drive, or the old 40 Arpent Road.

The St. Edward's School for Negroes was opened toward the end of 1918 by the Sisters of the Blessed Sacrament. It is co-educational.

In Jeanerette, the public school system began in 1885, and the first graduation exercises were held in 1902 for two young ladies. New school buildings have been erected to keep pace with the growth of the town. There were many private schools in Jeanerette; one still in existence is the school for boys and girls organized by the Sisters of Mercy in 1888. The first session began September 29, 1888. There were separate schools for the boys and girls until 1932 when the system became co-educational. The new school on the east side of Bayou Teche was occupied in September, 1959.

For the benefit of people unable to attend school during the day, the Free Night School was organized in the spring of 1898 by a few men in New Iberia. This school was maintained by voluntary contributions. In the fall of 1899 Mrs. Carrie Montagne was principal of the school, and Mrs. Percy Bennett taught mechanical drawing. The classes met in the High School building and had an enrollment of thirty-five at the beginning of the session. These night classes were continued for several years.

New Iberia was one of four towns which worked very hard to get the Industrial School which was to be built in the district. All the advantages of the town and parish were extolled; many meetings were held to devise ways and means to secure funds; benefit socials proved successful; a special tax was voted. But in the end New Iberia was disappointed. At the meeting of the Board of Trustees, called by Governor Murphy J. Foster, Lafayette was awarded the school. The Industrial School was later known as Southwestern Louisiana Institute and is today the University of Southwestern Louisiana.

In 1903, Ambroise Delcambre organized at Meadows a private school called the Delcambre Academy and later the Delcambre Commercial College. Meadows is today known as Delcambre. Forty-two pupils were enrolled at the beginning, and the total for the year was 153. A dormitory was built to house the many out-of-town students who were living in private homes. Military training, music, and commercial courses, among others, were offered. In January, 1905, Ambroise Delcambre suggested to the Vermilion Parish School Board that it appoint someone to teach in the Delcambre Commercial College. This proposition was accepted by the Board; and Telesmar Delcambre was named for the position. In 1906, the school interests were converted into a stock company. This company soon failed, and the Vermilion Parish School Board operated the school as a part of its system. Today the Delcambre school is administered by the Iberia Parish School Board.

Many newspapers have come and gone in the history of New Iberia. The issues of *The Confederate States*, May 18, 1864; *The Confederacy*, February 8, 1865; and *The Iberia Journal*, March 8, 1869, are most probably the earliest extant examples of papers published in New Iberia and are to be found in the library at Louisiana State University. The first two mentioned are printed on wallpaper. Some of the newspapers which published the official proceedings of the Police Jury were the *Iberia Times* in 1870, the *Iberia Banner* in 1871, and the *Banner and Courier* in 1872. The *Banner and Courier* was an English and French weekly founded in 1870. The *Louisiana Sugar Bowl*, at one time the official parish journal, also began in 1870 and was published at least until March 27, 1879. Governor W. P. Kellogg sent notice to the Police Jury that the *Iberia Progress*, a weekly founded in 1871, was to be the official paper for the parish of Iberia.

The *Iberia Statesman*, another French and English weekly established in 1871, was said to be the leading Republican paper in Southwest Louisiana; it had a circulation of 500 colored readers and a large number of whites. Four hundred subscribers read only the French side. This paper was the official journal of the state and parish. The New Iberia *Enterprise* purchased the press and type of the *Star*, another paper established in New Iberia not long after the close of the Civil War. The *Star* stopped publication for a while and was revived in 1880 for a few years. The New Iberia *Enterprise* was a weekly published from 1885 and until far into the twentieth century. *Le Pilote du Teche*, which seems to have been published only in English, was founded in Jeanerette in 1887. The New Iberia *Democrat*, 1890-1893, was originated to fight the Louisiana Lottery and expressed its opinion regardless of who stood in the way. In the 1890's the *Daily Iberian* began publication at three different times. The *Weekly Iberian* began publication in 1893 and continued as such until August 5, 1945 when it became the *Daily Iberian* which is still serving the community.

There were many other newspapers besides these mentioned. In general they carried local, state, national, and international news and provided articles on general information such as agriculture, health, and education, together with commercial and professional advertisements and amusing anecdotes.

Iberia Parish had no public library until the twentieth century, but at one time it did have a Public Reading Room, which came into being in 1896 and was centrally located on Main Street. This reading room provided the latest and best literature of the day as well as games such as chess and checkers; it was open without charge to the public. Expenses were met by benefits, such as the "Lawn Fete" given in May, 1898. The Reading Room was closed in December, 1898, as the funds were insufficient for the needs. After the belongings were sold and the debts paid, the excess money was given to the Knights of

Temperance, who had organized a club and planned to have a reading room.

About 1918 members of the First Methodist Church had a Sunday School Library for the children. The demand for books was so great that the Library was then opened on additional days. Then it was decided to invite a member of each church congregation in the city to form a board. This was done; and, about 1921, Miss Alma Sharp became the first librarian.

From this the Iberia Parish Library has developed. The building for the Iberia Parish Library on Weeks Street was built, in 1939, by donations from individuals and organizations. One group which made a substantial contribution was the Young Men's Business Club. The land was donated by the Iberia Parish School Board. For one year, 1947, the State Library took over and demonstrated how the library could be operated as a public responsibility. The following year, by popular vote, the library came under the jurisdiction of the Iberia Parish Police Jury with the Iberia Parish Library Board in control of operations. At present there are six branches in the parish, (one for Negroes), and two bookmobiles.

Before 1838 the Catholics from New Iberia and the surrounding area attended church services in St. Martinville. Then early in 1838 St. Peter's Catholic Church was completed. Pride in their community had made the people want to break away from the apron strings of St. Martinville. The lumber for the church was obtained from mills in the swamps, and the bricks were made from clay behind the Frederick Duperier home, which is now the property of Mt. Carmel Convent. In 1858 the building was lengthened by twenty feet. On the same site, in 1888, a much larger church, in Victorian Gothic style of architecture, was begun. The dedication of this building took place in May, 1890. By 1953 a larger St. Peter's, in French Renaissance style, had been constructed and dedicated.

The First Methodist Church was organized in New Iberia in 1828 and a church was built on the corner of French and Washington Streets in 1845. In 1860 the church proved too small, and another was built on the corner of Iberia and Washington Streets. This was burned on May 24, 1890, and in 1892 the cornerstone was laid for a new brick building located on Jefferson and St. Peter Streets. A fire partially destroyed this edifice which was restored and the first service after repairs was held October 13, 1907.

The Church of the Epiphany was the next to be organized in 1852. The church, of generally Gothic design, was consecrated in 1858 by General Leonidas Polk, the first Episcopal Bishop of Louisiana. During the time of occupation by the Federals, the church was used as a military hospital and guardhouse. A complete restoration of the building was made in 1960.

The colored people erected a number of churches before the turn of the century. The first, in 1869, was the Star Pilgrim Bapist Church, located in New Iberia. Next, in 1879, came the Boynton Chapel for the Methodists in Hubertville.

The other communities had their churches too. Since these were mostly Catholic communities, the churches were of that denomination. In Patoutville there was the St. Nicholas Church, erected in 1868; St. Joseph's Church in Loreauville, in 1873; St. John the Evangelist Church in Jeanerette, in 1879; and Our Lady of the Lake in Delcambre, in 1897.

The Presbyterians formed a congregation in 1895. Their first church building was begun in 1896 and was opened for service in May, 1898. Since 1957 their church has been on North Lewis Street.

The Jewish congregation was organized in New Iberia on April 26, 1897. By 1905 it had its synagogue. Among those instrumental in forming the Jewish congregation, "Gates of Prayer," and in erecting the synagogue, were Joseph H. Wise, Leon Dreyfus, Max Levy, Lazarre Kling, Morris Scharff, Sam Weil, Charles Kahn, Jake Weil, L. Wormser, A. Silverman, Louis Ochs, and Charles Gugenheim.[1] As early as 1885 the Jews of New Iberia boasted of their B'nai B'rith.

In recent years additional churches have been built for the growing congregations and for the members of other organizations. The Baptists were organized in 1926; and the Assembly of God, and the Church of Christ came later.

Charitable work was done in the community through the

---

[1]It is not known who were the first Jews in New Iberia or when they came. From the files of the New Iberia *Enterprise* we do know of one family who lived here before 1885. It was that of Leopold Strauss.

churches and organizations. One organization noted for its good work and not connected with any church was the New Iberia Unsectarian Aid Society, which held its first meeting October 16,1890. Many benefit entertainments were given by this society, among which was a Charity Ball which netted a $39.00 profit. In 1899 there were twelve strong fraternal organizations with about 700 active members to help the sick, the needy, orphans, and widows.

Many organizations were for cultural and social improvement or solely for pleasure. The Friendly Association of New Iberia held its first meeting July 10, 1847, and had as its object the promotion of sociability and the improvement of its members. About 100 persons attended this meeting, with Dr. Alfred Duperier as one of the leaders. An organization which afforded pleasure to its large membership was the Teche Club. A literary club met weekly on Saturdays. The Chrisoforo Colombo Mutual Benevolent Association, which was an Italian society, usually sponsored celebrations on October 12th. The Creole Club, organized in Patoutville in 1889, gave an entertainment in 1890 which netted over $200, to be applied to their building fund. The Iberia Game Protection and Gun Club was a parish-wide organization, active in 1890, which had as one of its main purposes the protection of game. Among other such clubs was the Attakapas Turf Association, one of whose members, J. F. Miller, formerly of Norfolk, Virginia, imported race horses from England and had a mile-long race track on his land, where annual races attracted great attention.

Excursions seemed to be a big event in the lives of the people and are very frequently mentioned in the newspapers. Frequently these excursions were by boat. On July 4, 1898, for example, the steamer, *Bagasse*, and two large barges tied up at the wharf at New Iberia, where coffee, lemonade, ice cream, and gumbo were sold. It was stated that even people in mourning attended this celebration, as the proceeds were to be used for the soldiers of the district in the Spanish-American War. There were also many excursions by train. One mentioned was from Crowley to New Orleans.

In 1872 a baseball game between the St. Martinville club and New Iberia was looked upon, by a newspaper reporter, as a "dread encounter." Six years later, however, when mention was made of a game between the Attakapas and the Quicksteps, it was referred to as a "friendly match game."

Some other amusements mentioned in newspaper files were the horse races, held at Marcel Derouen's race course; interesting bicycle races, held in Iberia Park; and a party near Jeanerette, to which some young ladies and gentlemen went by skiff and enjoyed a "jolly wet time."

A July 4th celebration under the auspices of Company C conducted many games, staged a sham battle, and wound up in a brilliant ball at night.

At other times the circus came to town. The one in 1878 was said to be the best in years, and the attendance was large. One of its attractions was the Fire King, who ate fire, drew a hot iron across his tongue, and allowed a committee from the community to pour melted lead into his mouth. Truly these were feats to help forget troubles. Later the chautauqua, both educational and entertaining, came yearly to instruct and amuse the people for a week or two.

The Carnival period was time for celebration. In 1888 it was sponsored by the Iberia Guards. If one may judge from the newspapers, the Carnival of 1896 was one of the best ever held in New Iberia. On the first page of the Carnival issue were the pictures of the officers of the Carnival Association and the sketches of the seven floats. Captions pointed out the significance of each float. On the next two pages were large drawings of these floats and a picture of their designer and decorator. Other pages contained a proclamation from his Majesty the King, descriptions of the costumes worn by the members of the court, and many advertisements. This publication was a souvenir edition. Today there are, in New Iberia, no formal parades for Carnival. However, there are two social groups the Krewe of Iberians (1948) and the Krewe of Andalusia (1957); each of which in season sponsors a bal masque which carries out an elaborate theme.

Plays, operas, and concerts were always welcome in the parish. On November 30, 1871, Thespian Hall was opened to the public with the plays "Lend Me Five Shillings" and "Stage Struck Yankee." On February 10, 1888, the opera "Rosita" came to New

Iberia. It was the first time this opera was presented in the South. The Spanish melodies were accompanied by guitar, tambourine, and castanets. The 1890-1891 season opened at the Iberia Opera House with "A Brave Woman," which was under the management of an ex-townsman. The leading lady had been born, educated, and married in New Iberia. The musical comedy "Wild Oats," with Oscar Sison and a good road company, was in New Iberia October 5, 1890. The same month Lillian Lewis played in "Credit Lorraine." Alexandre Dumas' "Count of Monte Cristo" and "Son of Monte Cristo" were presented by the actor Frank Lindon. For a week Jennie Holman played nightly. In 1897 Mlle. Lassen gave a concert in New Iberia and made the town her headquarters while she filled nearby engagements.

The official program of the Opera House in New Iberia was *The Stage*. It was, at first, one page, then a four-page combination of program and advertising. At each issue at least one thousand copies were printed. The program was distributed at all performances in the Opera House, to the offices and business places, and to the homes of Iberians. With the enlarging of the program, jokes, family news items, legal news, and social notes were added. Inch-high type was used in advertising the important events. The publication eventually became a ten-page weekly newspaper. It went out of publication in 1892 or 1893. The first *Daily Iberian*, founded in 1893, is considered a direct descendant of *The Star*, since E. F. Millard printed both publications.

As a result of fires, New Iberia had many opera houses. One of the first buildings used for stage entertainments was Thespian Hall; then there was Serett's Theatre, on the northeast corner of Main and Serett. Serett's was destroyed by fire sometime around the late 1880's. For a while after this, there were two opera houses in New Iberia: Veasey's Opera House, renamed the Vendome in 1901, on the Serett site; and the Athenaeum known later as the Iberia Opera House located on Main Street where the Hotel Frederick stands today. The Vendome and Iberia Opera House were competitors. The Iberia was larger and attracted more people. In 1898, the Iberia Opera House was destroyed by fire, and the Vendome met the same fate in 1905. It was not until about 1907 that the Elks Theatre was built, and New Iberia again had a well-planned building for plays and entertainments. The Elks Theatre, under the management of Julius Scharff, opened with a play on November 18th.

Records show that in season, from fall until spring, one opera house would have as many as thirty-four scheduled productions. As a special feature the first moving pictures for the public were held at the Elks Theatre on December 23, 1907. The movies shown were "The Inexperienced Chauffeur," "Zims, the Artist," "The Creditor's Prey," and "The Adventurous Auto Trip."

In 1897 the erection of an opera house was begun in Jeanerette. The name of the Jeanerette Opera House is noted in a 1908 issue of a newspaper.

Other forms of amusements for the people were parish fairs, street fairs, band concerts, races, skating at the skating rink, lodges with planned programs, and church entertainments.

The Church of the Epiphany had annually, beginning in 1877 and continuing for at least twenty years, a grand tournament with parades, contests and other amusements, and knights in colorful costumes. A queen was always crowned by the champion of the contests.

There were club houses, for members of social groups, located on Spanish Lake. At one time there were at least three clubs being patronized. Today there are country clubs, civic clubs, political, religious, and other social organizations.

Modern Iberia Parish has two festivals each fall. The Shrimp Festival is held in Delcambre with the blessing of the shrimp fleet. New Iberia holds the Sugar Cane Festival, an event which includes parades and an agricultural fair with varied exhibits.

New Iberia and Jeanerette both have City Parks. The New Iberia City Park is the location for the New Iberia Community Center, which sponsors teen-age programs. The Golden Age Club also uses the Center for its meetings. There is a swimming pool in the park, and there is also a pool for the colored in West End Park, located on Field Street.

Two radio broadcasting stations are located in New Iberia: KANE, since 1946 and KVIM, since 1951.

New Iberia had ready for service, in 1960, a new large modern parish hospital, and, in 1961, Consolata Home for the old folks. The parish has had many distinguished and interesting visitors. Among these was President Grover Cleveland, who spent several weeks with Joseph Jefferson at Jefferson's island home in 1893 and again in 1895. The great actor Edwin Booth also visited at the home of Jefferson. William L. Wilson, West Virginia Congressman, who introduced the bill that became known as the Wilson-Gorman Tariff, visited in New Iberia for several days in April, 1894. He was a guest for a few hours in the home of C. T. Cade. He also visited Avery Island. For the benefit of the New Iberia High School, Eugene V. Debs came to town to deliver an address in 1903. (The press noted that the laboring element did not attend his lecture.) In January, 1897, William Jennings Bryan spoke from the platform of the train when it stopped in New Iberia. At least a thousand persons greeted him. In May, 1901, President William McKinley stood on the platform of the last car and waved as his train passed through town. In February, 1903, Theodore Roosevelt's daughter, Alice, and her friend, Edith Root, the daughter of Elihu Root, visited the McIlhenny and Avery families on the island. The newspaper commented that Alice Roosevelt played the mandolin and banjo, and was inimitable at singing popular coon songs. President Theodore Roosevelt, who was a personal friend of John A. McIlhenny, (they were together in the Rough Rider Regiment in the Spaninsh American War) visited McIlhenny on Avery Island in October, 1907. In 1912, on his last visit to Louisiana, the President spoke both in French and in English, in front of the Iberia Parish Court House. Another visitor was Al Jolson, who sang here. This was before Mr. Jolson had gained fame.

Among the stories that have been handed down with the history of New Iberia is that of Emma Mille, who was the second wife of Dr. Alfred Duperier. She was at Last Island or Isle Derniere, when the terrible storm broke on August 10, 1856. The whole island was flooded with at least five feet of water. Not a single building withstood the storm. The lives lost numbered 182. Dr. Alfred Duperier, helping with the rescue of survivals, found Emma Mille floating on a log. She was the only survivor of her family. Dr. Duperier took the young girl, on the boat, the *Ingomar*, to his home to recuperate. The following year they were married. Mrs. Duperier was an accomplished pianist.

In her long life of about 99 years she never overcame her horror of bad weather.

This story, copied from a newspaper of 1886, appeared in the *Atlanta Constitution*. At a church service in New Iberia an attendant, Mr. Lewis, visibly showed his disbelief at a statement made by the preacher. At this the minister directed his remarks to the irreverent listener, who continued to curl his lip. The minister became scandalized at the conduct of Lewis and called upon the Almighty to punish the infidel by striking him with a bolt of lightning. The next day there was a thunderstorm and Mr. Lewis was seen walking down the street with about a dozen steel rods strapped to his body. The points of the rods formed a circle around his head. Lewis went to the preacher's house, where he found the good man praying and blinking at the flashes of lightning. Lewis laid his hand on the minister's shoulder. The movement and the sight of Lewis greatly startled the minister and, realizing his danger, the minister, with an agonized cry of terror fled to the back yard.

Dudley Avery told of one of the most exciting episodes of his life. During a thunderstorm, which came up suddenly, Mr. Avery took shelter under a blacksmith's shed which was near a building in which was stored 10,000 pounds of dynamite. Suddenly Avery felt a shock and saw the blacksmith going up in the air passing through the roof. The blacksmith was not getting farther away from Mr. Avery; Mr. Avery, too, was going up for thirty or forty feet. They came down with a rush and with their lungs in a state of collapse. The blacksmith was badly hurt; Avery escaped with a few stratches. Where the storehouse had stood was a hole thirty feet deep and sixty feet wide. The trees in the vicinity were burned black; and an oak tree, with a trunk two feet in diameter which had stood twenty feet from the building had been blown to shreds so fine that no part could be found.

One of the well known colored persons in New Iberia was Chauncey Depew, who called himself the champion boot black. He drove a hack, met all the trains, and welcomed every one to the city. Among Chauncey's audiences were many wide-eyed children who watched as he rattled the bones and jigged, hoping to get a few nickles for his entertainment. Chauncey became blind and lived to a ripe old age.

Dia Ambroise, colored, was another well known and loved member of the community. She was always kind and was happy to assist others at any time. Dia worked for more than forty years for Mrs. Leon Dreyfus. For many years she resided at 108 Taylor Street in a small home provided for her by the children of the Hayem Gougenheims. She had many friends who visited her. She was always a guest of Mrs. Dreyfus for her birthday dinner. She was more than 106 years old when she died in 1955.

In August, 1902, the first automobile in New Iberia arrived by freight train. It belonged to Dr. J. W. K. Shaw. When the doctor went out for a trial run, he was followed and cheered by the boys of the town.

The Fais-do-do, a Cajun term, is a country dance. The people in this section have always enjoyed dancing. Couples with small children, continued to go to these country dances, since a room was provided for the children, who would sleep while the parents danced. Fais-do-do means "go to sleep."

"Cajun," a corruption of the word "Acadian" was at first used with reference to the Acadians but years later and for a long time it meant an uneducated or possibly uncouth person generally from the country. The word today has its original meaning. The Cajuns usually lived a simple life and were satisfied with little so it is possible that this brought about the later meaning of the word Cajun. These people were, however, generally hardworkers and good people.

English is, of course, the official and ordinary language of the parish. French was spoken by the early settlers, the Acadians brought their idiomatic French, then the Spanish came with their mother-tongue. Even under Spanish rule French became the dominant language. With the coming of the Americans and the Louisiana Purchase the English language gradually took over. For many years after the Louisiana Purchase the three languages could be heard in this area. The descendants of the early Spaniards have discontinued the use of their language. English and French continued to be used legally and by the people generally for a long time. Although many people have not learned to use the French language it can often be heard in a variety of dialects throughout the parish.

The Bazus Hotel was a leading one in its day and famous for its good meals. For years it was the custom of those who roomed there to make coffee under a tree on Sunday morning. Friends from the town joined the group for a social hour. Later the hotel became a sort of refuge for homeless people.

The history of Iberia Parish brings to memory the kind of gracious hospitality that was found in the community; yet we must not forget the simple, industrious lives of the majority of the inhabitants. There was a full life for all, whether it was one of stock raising, farming, trade, or manufacturing. In each life there were heartaches and pleasures, and each life shared in the growth of the traditions and culture of Iberia Parish.

EPILOGUE

The facts set forth in the preceding chapters are responsible, to a large extent, for the opinions shared by visitors to the parish as well as by newcomers (a term used by the natives to designate a resident of less than one generation, sometimes two). The term "colorful," used with respect to the people and the surroundings, has been much overworked; but no other expression seems to capture so well the spirit of the descendants of the French, Spanish, and Acadian pioneers. Their ability to laugh at themselves is only one example of their "joie de vivre." Unlike the residents of the central and northern parishes of the state, the Iberians — whether working or playing — are a people in constant pursuit of pleasure. To the visitor this approach to living may at first seem Hedonistic; but, in time — like those who drop the coins in the famous fountain of Trevi in Rome, the visitor invariably returns. There is a saying among the people that one who has "tasted bayou water" is fated to return to the source — the Teche Country.

Politically Iberia Parish is in the third Congressional District of Louisiana, a section which has on several occasions reflected its conservatism by voting Republican in presidential elections. (The recent death of Mr. J. Paulin Duhe has deprived the Republican party in Louisiana of one of its staunchest supporters and leaders.) Ethnically, the 1960 census shows that approximately 71.4% of the parish population is white and 28.6% is Negro. About 70% of the residents of the parish are Catholic, 30% are Protestant, and less than 1% are Jewish.

In the past few decades, the oil industry has increased the population of Iberia Parish considerably. Many of the oil people have come from Texas and Mississippi; and they have effected some changes in the section's economy. The Naval Air Station at New Iberia, with its frequently shifting personnel and large payroll, has also affected the area. Young eligible males at the station are still young but no longer eligible: they have been married to the Teche Country by virtue of matrimony with one of the local girls. Family ties being what they are in Iberia Parish, it is certain that these young men will eventually find their way back to the bayou country with their families.

APPENDIX

APPENDIX

Sheriffs of Iberia Parish

Nov.	8, 1868	James Griswell	appointed
June	18, 1869	George Stubinger	appointed
Dec.	11, 1869	Clermont Young	appointed
Nov.	17, 1872	Allen Louis Hayes	appointed
Nov.	7, 1876	Theogene Viator	elected
Mar.	22, 1884	P. A. Veazey	elected
	1888	A. G. Barnard	elected
	1892	C. T. Cade	elected
	1900	George Henderson	elected
	1916	P. A. Landry	elected
	1940	Gilbert Ozenne	elected
	1950	Mrs. Gilbert Ozenne	appointed
	1952	J. Nick deRouen	elected
	1956	G. Jerry Wattigny	elected

Mayors of New Iberia

1876	Jasper Gall
1876-1878	Clement Young
1878-1884	J. L. Burke
1884-1887	Seraphin Boudreaux
1887-1889	August Erath
1889-1891	John Emmer
1891-1893	Julius Koch
1893-1895	William R. Burke
1895-1899	John Fisher
1899-1901	John Broussard
1901-1903	John Fisher
1903-1905	Jules E. Dupuy
1905-1909	C. C. Laughlin
1909-1913	J. S. Powers
1913-1915	Alphe Fontelieu (died in office)
1915-1921	H. S. Sealy
1921-1929	Edward LaSalle
1929-1940	Joe Daigre
1940-1944	William Lourd
1944-	P. A. Viator

Mayors of Jeanerette

Joseph Edmond Provost
Joseph Alcide Provost
George H. Ring
Gerald Stiges

F. M. Welch
George P. Minvielle
L. A. Moresi
H. L. Bracey
Joseph F. Moore
L. A. Moresi
John M. Durocher
F. J. Gaiennie
F. J. Druilhet
S. J. Bourgeois
Neil Jeffrey
E. L. Chaney
J. P. Lapeyrouse
Curtis J. Myers

Mayors of Delcambre

1907-1909	Pierre Pelloat
	Desire Delcambre (Mayor Pro Tem)
1909-1911	Alphe Leleux (First election April 19, 1910)
1911-1916	Jos. A. Leblanc
1916-1924	Fernand Landry
1924-1926	Sulie Leblanc
1926-1936	Edvar J. Leblanc
1936-1944	J. V. Delcambre
1944-1948	E. J. Hymel
1948-1951	Wiltz Landry
1952-	Euda Delcambre

Mayors of Loreauville

Charles Fernes Berard
Eugene Prince
Dr. Guy Shaw
Charles Mestayer
Husville Gonsoulin
Aymar LeBlanc
J. E. Broussard
Arthur Snow
Tony Berard
Sully Berard
Lawrence Ransonet
Forbus J. Mestayer, Sr.

Population
Iberia Parish-New Iberia-Jeanerette-Loreauville-Delcambre

					Iberia	Ver-milion
1785		125				
1788		190				
1789		177				
1848		300				
1850		306				
1860	(No record)					
1870	9,042	1,472				
1880	16,676	2,709	698			
1890	20,997	3,447	1,309			
1900	29,015	6,815	1,905			
1910	21,262	7,499	2,206	291	308	
1920	26,855	6,278	2,512	439	443	
1930	28,192	8,003	2,228	441	272-	369
1940	37,183	13,747	3,362	490	583-	672
1950	40,059	16,467	4,692	478	667-	796
1960	51,657	29,062	5,568	655	830-	1,027

Census, December, 1789, for New Iberia

	total in household
Jean Bte. Darby-Commandant	42
France de Bandera	5
Juan Guerero	4
Gabriel Lopez	4
Maria Lopez	3
Joe Fernandez	5
Anto. Fernandez	2
Felicia Lopez	3
Franco Segura	4
Gonsalo de Prados	4
Manuel de Prados	5
Julien de Aquilar	3
Miguel Romero	7
Juan Migues	4
Anto Villiatore	4
Bernido de Aponte	6
Franco Ortis	6
Frans Arevst	14
Lorenzo Dieppe	5
Jos Derouan	8
Jean Derouan	6
Adam Charles	2
Pierre Arman	4
Jaques Nope	9
Marte Pellerin	6
Louis Pellerin	4
Wm. Lagautray	8
total	177

A few entries taken from the *Brand Register*,
St. Martin Court House

Year	Name	Brand
1769	Claude Broussard	
1770	Pierre Dugat	
	Lacautray	
	J^n. A^to. Le Jeune	
	J. Beaulieu fils	
1770	Alexandre Dugat	
1770	Pierre Dugat fils	
1770	Joseph Drouen pere	
1770	Francois Grevemberg	
1777	Claude Duhon	
1780	B^te. Boute	
1780	Antonio Billatoro	
1781	Juan Migues	
1782	Joseph Romero	
1784	Domingo Domingues pere	
1785	Francois Segura	
1785	Jean Romere pere	
1787	Francois Gonsoulin	
1793	Michel Romere	
1797	Louis Deblanc pere	
1800	Joseph Olivier Devezin	
1802	Jacques Drouen pere	
1809	J^n. Pierre Decuirs	

TRANSLATION OF SPANISH DOCUMENTS

Translations of *Papeles Procedentes de Cuba* which are deposited in the Archivo General de Indias at Seville, Spain[2]

Legajo no. 576

Immigrant Families.—

List of persons who from Malaga boarded the brig *St. Joseph* with Captain Don Antonio Caballero, as follows:

On June 1, sixteen families consisting of eighty-two persons boarded ship and on the 13th of the same month disembarked in Cadiz by order of the President and from the 13th of this same month the Captain provided them daily with money until July 21, one child having died June 17.

On the afternoon of July 21 sixty-seven persons embarked in which were included the Master (or Chief Craftsman) of bleeding with his wife and one child who in family class are with Senor Don Antonio de Galvez.

On August 20 at 5:30 in the afternoon Joseph Villalba at the age of nine, died in Puerto Rico.

On September 9, sixty-seven persons landed in Habana to whom were supplied their daily expense for maintenance.

On October 3, Joseph Molina died at the hour of prayer.

On the afternoon of October 10, forty-four persons embarked to continue their journey to Louisiana and on the 14th in the afternoon it was necessary because of illness to put on land a family of three persons.

On the afternoon of October 29 Sebastian de Segura died and until now November 11, forty persons remain who have been maintained; New Orleans, November 15, 1778.—

By the Captain Caballero

Antonio Remon (rubricado)

---

[2]To retain their old-world charm of expression and exact meaning, the documents, furnished by Manuel Fuentes Mairena, are presented in a literal translation.

Juan Lopez.

I the undersigned scrivener of Our Lordship the King proclaim in all his kingdom and domains, resident of this city, certify and affirm that before me appeared Senor Don Joseph Ortega y Monrroy, priest of this same city, the deed whose contents are as follows:

Don Joseph de Ortega y Monrroy commissioned by His Majesty, may God guard Him, for the enrollment of families from the kingdom of the Granada Coast to the towns of Louisiana, and Juan Lopez Riveros native of Almachar and resident of the city of Malaga, of the parish of St. James, thirty-nine years old, of the farming class. We say and contract I the second one, that ought to pass in person and that of my wife Maria Ruiz, thirty-five years old, native of Velez, Malaga and resident of Malaga and of my children Felix four years old, Rafael one year old, Francisca eleven years old, Pepa eight years old and my mother-in-law of more than fifty years, to establish in said towns to which we all go complying freely and willingly without force, violence or promise other than the share made to us in the name of His Majesty for which we will be disposed and readily go to the city of Malaga to embark and make the journey when the Senor Commissioner orders it, who will pay the cost of our maintenance from the day we leave our homes, and freight transportation, to our arrival in Louisiana is to the charge and account of your Majesty and in the same he will give us comfortable lodging, build us a house, assign land to us, supply us with live stock, utensils and implements for cultivating the lands, paying us the first sowing and assisting us with all the necessities of livelihood to the harvesting of our first crop from which time we will begin to subsist on our own and contribute to your Majesty that portion which is convenient to our situation to repay the cost of our travel and maintenance, keeping for our heirs the succession and perpetual possession of the house, lands and live stock which will be assigned to us with all the other things we acquire and will acquire in said town.

All of which obliges us to what is here mutually and reciprocally contained and each one will comply with the correspondent part and for that reason we sign this duplicate contract in the city of Malaga on July 23, 1777, the witnesses being Don Joseph de Torres, Don Juan Terron and Don Joaquin Pizarro and because none of the members of this family can sign their name, this was done for them by the witnesses Joaquin Pizarro, Juan Terron and Joseph de Torres. Dn Joseph de Ortega y Monrroy.

As the clear reference and appearance of the cited agent to whom I relinquish and returned the original to the named Senor Don Joseph de Ortega that he sign here his receipt and at his petition give this to be marked and signed in the city of Malaga on June 4, 1778.

Luis Vidal (seal)

Dn Joseph de Ortega y Monrroy (seal)

The scriveners of Our Lord the King, I publish and give the number of this city of Malaga which we here sign, certify and attest that Luis Vidal whose signature and seal appears on the preceding testimony is scrivener of Our Lord the King, proclaim in all his kingdom and domains, native of this city, faithful, loyal and worthy of confidence and as such uses and exercises his office and of his testimony and other writings have given him and do give entire attestation and credit and judgment and outside of it and so that it will be recorded where necessary we give the present one in the city of Malaga the 6th day of June, 1778.

Miguel Lopez Cuartero. Gregorio Martinez de Ribera
Manuel Joseph Romero (seal)

Joseph de Molina y Postigo.

I the undersigned scrivener of Our Lordship the King, proclaim in all His Kingdom and domains, resident of this city, certify and affirm that before me, Senor Don Joseph de Ortega y Monrroy, priest of this same city, the deed whose contents are as follows:

Don Joseph de Ortega y Monrroy commissioned by His Majesty, may God guard him, for the enrollment of families from the kingdom of Granada to the towns of Louisiana and Joseph de Molina y Postigo native and resident of the town of Macharaviaya fifty-eight years old and of the farming class: We say and we contract, I the second one that should pass in person and of my two sons, Luis native of the city of Malaga twenty-two years old and Antonio twenty years old and of the same said city to settle in said towns to which we go conformed, free and voluntarily without force, violence or promise other than the share made to us in the name of His Majesty for which we will be disposed and readily go and present ourselves in this city of Malaga to embark and make the journey when the Senor Commissioner orders it, who will pay the cost of our maintenance from the day we leave our homes freight transportation to our arrival in Louisiana is in the charge and account of Your Majesty and in the same he will give us comfortable lodging, build us a house, assign land to us, provide us with cattle, utensils and implements for cultivating and labor of the lands paying us the first sowing and assisting us with everything necessary for our livelihood to the harvesting of our first crop from which time we will begin to subsist on our own contributing to Your Majesty that portion which is convenient to our situation to repay the cost of our travel and maintenance, keeping for our heirs the succession and perpetual possession of the house, lands and live stock which will be assigned to us and all the other things we acquire and will acquire in said town.

All of which obliges us to what is here contained and each one of us will comply with the correspondent part and for that reason we sign this contract in the city of Malaga on July 26, 1777, the witnesses being Don Joseph de Torres, Dn Juan Terron and Dn Joaquin Pizarro and I sign for my sons, Luis and Antonio Postigo: Joseph de Molina, Joaquin Pizarro, Juan Terron, Joseph de Torres, Dn Joseph de Ortega y Monrroy.

As the clear reference and appearance of the cited agent to whom I relinquish and return the original to the named Don Joseph de Ortega that he sign here his receipt and at his petition give this to be sealed and signed in the city of Malaga, June 4, 1778.

Luis Vidal
Dn Joseph de Ortega y Monrroy
The scriveners of Our Lord the King. . . .

Juan Garrido.
I the undersigned scrivener of Our Lordship, the King, proclaim in all his kingdom and domains, resident of this city,

certify and affirm that before me appeared Senor Don Joseph
Ortega y Monrroy, priest of this same city, the deed whose contents are as follows:

Don Joseph de Ortega y Monrroy commissioned by His Majesty, may God guard him, for the enrollment of families from
the kingdom of the Granada Coast to the towns of Louisiana,
and Juan Garrido native of Alhaurin de la Torre, resident of
Malaga, forty years old and of the farming class, we say and
contract, I the second one, that ought to pass in person, and of
my wife Inez Maldonado, native of Pizarra, thirty-four years
old and my children Juan Garrido two years old, Sebastian Villalba eight years old, Catalina Villalba ten years, to settle in
said town and that we all go conformed, free and willingly without other force, violence or promise other than the share made
to us in the name of his Majesty for which we will be disposed
and readily go to the city of Malaga to embark and make the
journey when the said Commisioner orders it who will pay the
cost of our maintenance from the day we leave our homes, and
freight transportation to our arrival in Louisiana and that in
the same he will give us comfortable lodgings, build us a house,
assign lands to us, provide us with live stock, utensils and implements for cultivating and labor on the lands, paying us the
first sowing and assisting us with all the necessities of livelihood to the harvesting of the first crop from which time we
will begin to subsist on our own and contribute to Your Majesty
that portion which is convenient to our situation to repay the
cost of our travel and maintenance keeping for ourselves, our
heirs and successors, the possession and perpetual ownership
of the house, lands and live stock which will be assigned to us
with all the other things we acquire and will acquire in said
town.

All of which obliges us to what is here mutually and reciprocally contained and each one will comply with the correspondent
part and for that reason we sign this duplicate contract in the
city of Malaga on July 31, 1777. The witnesses being Don Joseph
de Torres, Don Juan Terron and Don Joaquin Pizarro.—Juan
Terron, Don Joseph de Ortega y Monrroy.

As the clear reference and appearance of the cited agent to

whom I relinquish and returned the original to the named Senor
Don Joseph de Ortega that he sign here his receipt and at his
petition give this to be sealed and signed in the city of Malaga
on the 4th day of the month of June, 1778.

Luis Vidal

Dn Joseph de Ortega y Monrroy
The scriveners of Our Lord the King. . . .

Julian Aguilar.

I the undersigned scrivener of Our Lordship, the King, proclaim in all his kingdom and domains, resident of this city,
certify and affirm that before me appeared Senor Don Joseph
Ortega y Monrroy, priest of this same city, the deed whose
contents are as follows:

Don Joseph de Ortega y Monrroy commissioned by His Majesty, may God guard him, for the enrollment of families from
the kingdom of the Granada Coast to the towns of Louisiana,
and Julian de Aguilar, native and resident of the city of Malaga
in the parish of the Holy Martyrs and twenty-eight years of
age, of the farming class, we say and contract, I the second one
that ought to pass in person and of my wife Francisca Duran
twenty-six years old, native of the same city and of my children
Francisco one year old and Ana eight years to settle in the said
towns to which we go conformed, free and voluntarily, without
any other force intervening, violence or promise other than that
of the share made to us in the name of His Majesty for which
we will be disposed and readily present ourselves in this city
of Malaga to embark and make the voyage as soon as the said
Senor Commissioner orders it who will pay the cost of our
maintenance from the day we leave our homes, and freight
transportation to our arrival in Louisiana and that in the same
he will give us comfortable lodgings, build us a house, assign
lands to us, provide us with live stock, utensils and implements
for cultivating and labor on the lands, paying us the first sowing and assisting us with all the necessities of livelihood to the
harvesting of the first crop from which time we will begin to
subsist on our own and contribute to Your Majesty that portion
which is convenient to our situation to repay the cost of our
travel and maintenance keeping for ourselves, our heirs and

successors, the possession and perpetual ownership of the house, lands and live stock which will be assigned to us with all the other things we acquire and will acquire in said town.

All of which obliges us to what is here mutually and reciprocally contained and each one will comply with the correspondent part and for that reason we sign this duplicate contract in the city of Malaga on August 8, 1777, the witnesses being Don Juan Terron, Don Joaquin Pizarro, Don Joseph de Torres and I sign for all in my family, Julian de Aguilar, Juan Torres, Joachin Pizarro, Joseph de Torres, Dn Joseph de Ortega y Monrroy.

As the clear reference and appearance of the cited agent to whom I relinquish and returned the original to the named Senor Don Joseph de Ortega that he sign here his receipt and at his petition give this to be sealed and signed in the city of Malaga on the 4th day of the month of June, 1778.

Luis Vidal

Dn Joseph de Ortega y Monrroy
The scriveners of Our Lord, the King. . . .

Francisco Moreno.

I the undersigned scrivener of Our Lordship, the King, proclaim in all his kingdom and domains, resident of this city, certify and affirm that before me appeared Senor Don Joseph Ortega y Monrroy, priest of this same city, the deed whose contents are as follows:

Don Joseph de Ortega y Monrroy commissioned by His Majesty, may God guard him, for the enrollment of families from the kingdom of the Granada Coast to the towns of Louisiana, and Francisco Moreno, native and resident of the city of Malaga, in the parish of St. John, forty-six years old and of the farming class, we say and contract, I the second one, that ought to pass in person, that of my wife Ana Lorenza Mancebo, forty years old and my children, Francisco fourteen years, Fernando twelve years, Ana seventeen years, Josefa sixteen years, Maria ten years, to settle in said towns to which we all go conformed, free and voluntarily, without other force, violence or promise than that of the share made to us in the name of His Majesty for which we will be disposed and readily present ourselves in this city of Malaga to embark and make our journey as soon as the said Senor Commissioner orders it who will pay the cost of our maintenance from the day we leave our homes, and freight transportation to our arrival in Louisiana and that in the same he will give us comfortable lodgings, build us a house, assign lands to us, provide us with live stock, utensils and implements for cultivating and labor on the lands, paying us the first sowing and assisting us with all the necessities of livelihood to the harvesting of the first crop from which time we will begin to subsist on our own and contribute to Your Majesty that portion which is convenient to our situation to repay the cost of our travel and maintenance keeping for ourselves, our heirs and successors, the possession and perpetual ownership of the house, lands and livestock which will be assigned to us with all the other things we acquire and will acquire in said town.

All of which obliges us to what is here mutually and reciprocally contained and each one will comply with the correspondent part and for that reason we sign this duplicate contract in the city of Malaga on August 1, 1777, and because I cannot write my signature, one of the witnesses who was present did it for me, Don Joseph de Torres, Don Juan Terron and Don Joaquin Pizarro and he signed for all the interested members of this family. Joaquin Pizarro, Juan Terron and Joseph de Torres, Don Joseph de Ortega y Monrroy.

As the clear reference and appearance of the cited agent to whom I relinquish and returned the original to the named Senor Don Joseph de Ortega that he sign here his receipt and at his petition give this to be sealed and signed in the city of Malaga on the 4th day of the month of June, 1778.

Luis Vidal

Dn Joseph de Ortega y Monrroy

The scriveners of Our Lord the King. . . .

Gonzalo de Prados.

I the undersigned scrivener of Our Lordship, the King, proclaim in all his kingdom and domains, resident of this city, certify and affirm that before me appeared Senor Don Joseph Ortega y Monrroy, priest of this same city, the deed whose contents are as follows:

Don Joseph de Ortega y Monrroy commissioned by His Maj-

Flood at New Iberia. Persons being brought to St. Peter's Catholic Church to attend Mass on May 29, 1927.

Lallande's store May 26, 1927, when the flood waters first swept into New Iberia.

Aerial View of Spanish Lake near New Iberia.

Typical scene at a modern sugar mill.

Aerial view of Naval Air Station in Iberia Parish.

esty, may God guard him, for the enrollment of families from the kingdom of the Granada Coast to the towns of Louisiana, and Gonzalo de Prados native and resident of the city of Malaga in the parish of St. James, thirty-six years of age of the farming class, we say and contract, I the second one that ought to pass in person, that of my wife, Teresa Guzman thirty-eight years native of the same city and my children, Manuel fourteen years, Maria eleven, Gertrudis nine years old and Theresa three years to settle in said towns to which we all go conformed, free and voluntarily, without any other force intervening, violence or promise other than that of the share made to us in the name of His Majesty for which we will be disposed and readily present ourselves in this city of Malaga to embark and make the voyage as soon as the said Senor Commissioner orders it who will pay the cost of our maintenance from the day we leave our homes, and freight transportation to our arrival in Louisiana and that in the same he will give us comfortable lodgings, build us a house, assign lands to us, provide us with live stock, utensils and implements for cultivating and labor on the lands, paying us the first sowing and assisting us with all the necessities of livelihood to the harvesting of the first crop from which time we will begin to subsist on our own and contribute to Your Majesty that portion which is convenient to our situation to repay the cost of our travel and maintenance keeping for ourselves, our heirs and successors, the possession and perpetual ownership of the house, lands and live stock which will be assigned to us with all the other things we acquire and will acquire in said town.

All of which obliges us to what is here mutually and reciprocally contained and each one will comply with the correspondent part and for that reason we sign this duplicate contract in the city of Malaga on August 7, 1777. The witnesses being Don Joseph de Torres, Don Juan Terron and Joaquin Pizarro and because none of the interested persons of this family know how to sign their names this was done for them by the witness Joaquin Pizarro, Juan Torres, Joseph de Torres, Don Joseph de Ortega y Monrroy.

As the clear reference and appearance of the cited agent to whom I relinquish and returned the original to the named Senor

Don Joseph de Ortega that he sign here his receipt and at his petition give this to be sealed and signed in the city of Malaga on the 4th day of the month of June, 1778.

Luis Vidal
Don Joseph de Ortega y Monrroy
The scriveners of our Lord the King. . . .

Fernando Ibañes.

I the undersigned scrivener of Our Lordship, the King, proclaim in all his kingdom and domains, resident of this city, certify and affirm that before me appeared Senior Don Joseph Ortega y Monrroy, priest of this same city, the deed whose contents are as follows:

Don Joseph de Ortega y Monrroy commissioned by His Majesty, may God guard him, for the enrollment of families from the kingdom of the Granada Coast to the towns of Louisiana, and Fernando Ibañes, native of the place Caraveos, Archbishopric of Burgos, and of the farming class, we say and contract, I the second one that ought to pass in person and that of my wife Dona Maria Cabrera native of the town of Macharavialla and resident of the city of Malaga, thirty-five years old, and that of my children, Fernando seven years old, Joseph six years, Antonio one and one-half years, Fernando one month and Maria four years to settle in said towns to which we all go conformed, free and voluntarily without other force, violence or promise other than the share made to us in the name of His Majesty, for which we will be disposed and readily present outselves in this city of Malaga to embark and make the journey as soon as the said Senor Commissioner orders it who will pay the cost of our maintenance from the day we leave our homes, and freight transportation to our arrival in Louisiana and that in the same he will give us comfortable lodgings, build us a house, assign lands to us, provide us with live stock, utensils and implements for cultivating and labor on the lands, paying us the first sowing and assisting us with all the necessities of livelihood to the harvesting of the first crop from which time we will begin to subsist on our own and contribute to Your Majesty that portion which is convenient to our situation to repay the cost of our travel and maintenance keeping for ourselves, our heirs and successors, the possession and perpetual ownership of the house, lands and livestock which will be assigned to us with all the other things we acquire and will acquire in said town.

All of which obliges us to what is here mutually and reciprocally contained and each one will comply with the correspondent part and for that reason we sign this duplicate contract in the city of Malaga on August 24, 1777, the witnesses being Don Joseph de Torres, Don Joaquin Pizarro and Don Antonio Soler and signed for him, his wife and children. Antonio Soler, Fernando Ibanez, Antonio Soler, Joaquin Pizarro, Don Joseph de Ortega y Monrroy.

As the clear reference and appearance of the cited agent to whom I relinquish and returned the original to the named Senor Don Joseph de Ortega that he sign here his receipt and at his petition give this to be sealed and signed in the city of Malaga on the 4th day of the month of June, 1778.

Luis Vidal

Don Joseph de Ortega y Monrroy
   The scriveners of Our Lord the King. . . .

Juan Migues.

I the undersigned scrivener of Our Lordship, the King, proclaim in all his kingdom and domains, resident of this city, certify and affirm that before me appeared Senor Don Joseph Ortega y Monrroy, priest of this same city, the deed whose contents are as follows:

Don Joseph de Ortega y Monrroy commissioned by His Majesty, may God guard him, for the enrollment of families from the kingdom of the Granada Coast to the towns of Louisiana, and Juan Migues, native of San Salvador de Febra, Bishopric of Tuy, and resident of the city of Malaga, the parish of San Juan, thirty years old, of the farming class, we say and contract, I, the second one that I have to pass in person, that of my wife, Salvadora de Quero native of this city twenty-five years old and my children, Joseph twelve years, Salvador one year and Salvador de Quero my wife's brother, fifteeen years old, to settle in said towns, that we all go conformed, free and voluntarily without other force, violence or promise other than that of the share made to us in the name of His Majesty, for which we will be disposed and readily present ourselves in this city of Malaga to embark and make the voyage as soon as the said Senor Commissioner orders it, who will pay the cost of our maintenance from the day we leave our homes, and freight transportation to our arrival in Louisiana and that in the same he will give us comfortable lodgings, build us a house, assign lands to us, provide us with live stock, utensils and implements for cultivating and labor on the lands, paying us the first sowing and assisting us with all the necessities of livelihood to the harvesting of the first crop from which time we will begin to subsist on our own and contribute to Your Majesty that portion which is convenient to our situation to repay the cost of our travel and maintenance keeping for ourselves, our heirs and successors, the possession and perpetual ownership of the house, lands and live stock which will be assigned to us with all the other things we acquire and will acquire in said town.

All of which obliges us to what is here mutually and reciprocally contained and each one will comply with the correspondent part and for that reason we sign this duplicate contract in the city of Malaga on January 15, 1778, the witnesses being Don Joaquin Pizarro, Don Diego Terron and Don Antonio Soler. Signed for himself and all, Juan Migues. Antonio Soler, Diego Terron, Joaquin Pizarro, Don Joseph de Ortega y Monrroy.

Note—Because of the death of Salvador de Quero, Gregorio Gonzalez, native of Mijas, thirty years old, cousin of Salvadora was sent in his place. Ortega.

Another—Because of the exhortation of the Cura of the town of Churriana, Gregorio Gonzalez was not permitted to embark, because he had contracted a betrothal to Maria Garcia, native of his parish so in place of this one another relative of the family, Joseph de Porras, native and resident of the town of Cartama, forty years of age went instead. Malaga, June 3, 1778. Ortega.

Another—In going over the list of individuals of the sixteen families who were embarked, Joseph Migues was missing, and because of the favorable weather for navigating, the brig set sail without this said individual. Malaga, June 5, 1778. Ortega.

As the clear reference and appearance of the cited agent to whom I relinquish and returned the original to the named Senor

Don Joseph de Ortega that he sign here his receipt and at his petition give this to be sealed and signed in the city of Malaga on the 4th day of the month of June, 1778.

Luis Vidal
Don Joseph de Ortega y Monrroy
The scriveners of Our Lord the King. . . .

Sebastian de Segura.

I the undersigned scrivener of Our Lordship, the King, proclaim in all his kingdom and domains, resident of this city, certify and affirm that before me appeared Senor Don Joseph Ortega y Monrroy, priest of this same city, the deed whose contents are as follows:

Don Joseph de Ortega y Monrroy commissioned by His Majesty, may God guard him, for the enrollment of families from the kingdom of the Granada Coast to the towns of Louisiana, and Sebastian de Segura, native and resident of the city of Malaga of the parish St. James, twenty-eight years old, of the farming class, we say and contract, I the second one who am to pass in my person, that of my wife, Antonia de Castilla, native of this city, twenty-four years old and of my son Francisco, two years old, to settle in said towns to which we all go conformed, free and voluntarily, without other force, violence or promise other than that of the share made to us in the name of His Majesty for which we will be disposed and readily present ourselves in this city of Malaga to embark and make the voyage as soon as the said Senor Commissioner orders it who will pay the cost of our maintenance from the day we leave our homes, and freight transportation to our arrival in Louisiana and that in the same he will give us comfortable lodgings, build us a house, assign lands to us, provide us with live stock, utensils and implements for cultivating and labor on the lands, paying us the first sowing and assisting us with all the necessities of livelihood to the harvesting of the first crop from which time we will begin to subsist on our own and contribute to Your Majesty that portion which is convenient to our situation to repay the cost of our travel and maintenance keeping for ourselves, our heirs and successors, the possession and perpetual ownership of the house, lands and live stock which will be assigned to us with all the other things we acquire and will acquire in said town.

All of which obliges us to what is here mutually and reciprocally contained and each one will comply with the correspondent part and for that reason we sign this duplicate contract in the city of Malaga on February 9, 1778, the witnesses being Don Joaquin Pizarro, Don Diego Terron and Don Antonio Soler. Sebastian Segura, Antonia Castilla, Antonio Soler, Joaquin Pizarro, Diego Terron, Don Joseph de Ortega y Monrroy.

As the clear reference and appearance of the cited agent to whom I relinquish and returned the original to the named Senor Don Joseph de Ortega that he sign here his receipt and at his petition give this to be sealed and signed in the city of Malaga on the 4th day of the month of June, 1778.

Luis Vidal
Don Joseph de Ortega y Monrroy
The scriveners of Our Lord the King. . . .

Joseph Artacho.

I the undersigned scrivener of Our Lordship, the King, proclaim in all his kingdom and domains, resident of this city, certify and affirm that before me appeared Senor Don Joseph Ortega y Monrroy, priest of this same city, the deed whose contents are as follows:

Don Joseph de Ortega y Monrroy commissioned by His Majesty, may God guard him, for the enrollment of families from the kingdom of the Granada Coast to the towns of Louisiana, and Joseph de Artacho, native of the town of Torrox, resident of the city of Malaga, the parish of St. James, thirty-six years old, of the farming class, we say and contract, I the second one who am to pass in my person, that of my wife Francisca Villegas thirty-five years old, from the same place and residence, and my children, Gregorio fourteen years old, Cristobal ten years, and Maria six years to settle in said towns to which we all go conformed, free and voluntarily without other force, violence or promise other than that of the share made to us in the name of His Majesty for which we will be disposed and readily present ourselves in this city of Malaga to embark and make the voyage as soon as the said Senor Commissioner orders it who will pay the cost of our maintenance from the day we leave our homes, and freight transportation to our arrival in Louisiana and that in the same he will give us comfortable lodgings, build us a house, assign lands to us, provide us with live stock, utensils and implements for cultivating and labor on the lands, paying us the first sowing and assisting us with all the necessities of livelihood to the harvesting of the first crop from which time we will begin to submit on our own and contribute to Your Majesty that portion which is convenient to our situation to repay the cost of our travel and maintenance keeping for ourselves, our heirs and successors, the possession and perpetual ownership of the house, lands and live stock which will be assigned to us with all the other things we acquire and will acquire in said town.

All of which obliges us to what is here mutually and reciprocally contained and each one will comply with the correspondent part and for that reason we sign this duplicate contract in the city of Malaga on April 10, 1778, the witnesses being Don Joaquin Pizarro, Don Diego Terron and Don Joseph Montenegros, and because none of the interested persons know how to sign their names it was done for them by the witness Joseph Montenegro, Diego Terron, Joaquin Pizarro, Don Joseps de Ortega y Monrroy.

As the clear reference and appearance of the cited agent to whom I relinquish and returned the original to the named Senor Don Joseph de Ortega that he sign here his receipt and at his petition give this to be sealed and signed in the city of Malaga on the 4th day of the month of June, 1778.

Luis Vidal

Don Joseph de Ortega y Monrroy
The scriveners of Our Lord the King. . . .

Antonio Villatoro.

I the undersigned scrivener of Our Lordship, the King, proclaim in all his kingdom and domains, residents of this city, certify and affirm that before me appeared Senor Don Joseph Ortega y Monrroy, priest of this same city, the deed whose contents are as follows:

Don Joseph de Ortega y Morroy commissioned by His

Majesty, may God guard him, for the enrollment of families from the kingdom of the Granada Coast to the towns of Louisiana, and Teresa Gomez, native and resident of the place of Alhaurin de la Torre, forty-six years old, widow and of the farming class, we say and contract, I the second, who am to pass in person and my children, Antonio Villatoro nineteen years old, Rita fifteen years, Maria thirteen years, Juana eleven years and my nephew Francisco Villatoro twenty-one years old, all of this said place and residency, to settle in said towns to which we all go conformed, free and voluntarily without other force, violence or promise other than that of the shares made to us in the name of His Majesty for which we will be disposed and readily present ourselves to make this voyage as soon as the said Senor Commissioner orders it who will pay the cost of our maintenance from the day we leave our homes, and freight transportation to our arrival in Louisiana and that in the same he will give us comfortable lodgings, build us a house, assign lands to us, provide us with live stock, utensils and implements for cultivating and labor on the lands, paying us the first sowing and assisting us with all the necessities of livelihood to the harvesting of the first crop from which time we will begin to subsist on our own and contribute to Your Majesty that portion which is convenient to our situation to repay the cost of our travel and maintenance keeping for ourselves, our heirs and successors, the possession and perpetual ownership of the house, lands and live stock which will be assigned to us with all the other things we acquire and will acquire in said town.

All of which obliges us to what is here mutually and reciprocally contained and each one will comply with the correspondent part and for that reason we sign this duplicate contract in the city of Malaga on February 24, 1778, the witnesses being Don Joaquin Pizarro, Don Diego Terron, and Don Antonio Soler, and signed for all of hers, Teresa Gomez. Antonio Soler, Joaquin Pizarro, Diego Terron, Don Joseph de Ortega y Monrroy.

Note—Attention—Rita Villatoro contracted matrimony with Juan Gonzalez, native of Alhaurin de la Torre, nineteeen years old so was included in this contract.

As the clear reference and appearance of the cited agent to

whom I relinquish and returned the original to the named Senor Don Joseph de Ortega that he sign here his receipt and at his petition give this to be sealed and signed in the city of Malaga on the 4th day of the month of June, 1778.

Luis Vidal

Don Joseph de Ortega y Monrroy
The scriveners of Our Lord the King. . . .

Francisco Ortiz.

I the undersigned scrivener of Our Lordship, the King, proclaim in all his kingodm and domains, resident of this city, certify and affirm that before me appeared Senor Don Joseph Ortega y Monrroy, priest of this same city, the deed whose contents are as follows:

Don Joseph de Ortega y Monrroy commissioned by His Majesty, may God guard him, for the enrollment of families from the kingdom of the Granda Coast to the towns of Louisiana, and Francisco de Ortiz, native and resident of the town of Mijas, thirty-two years old, of the farming class, we say and contract, I the second who am to pass in person, that of my wife Francisca Blanco of the same residency, thirty-one years old and my children Juan two years and Catalina six years, to settle in said towns to which we all go conformed, free and voluntarily without other force, violence or promise other than that of the shares made to us in the name of His Majesty for which we will be disposed and readily present ourselves in this city of Malaga to embark and make the voyage as soon as the said Senor Commissioner orders it who will pay the cost of our maintenance from the day we leave our homes, and freight transportation to our arrival in Louisiana and that in the same he will give us comfortable lodgings, build us a house, assign lands to us, provide us with live stock, utensils and implements for cultivating and labor on the lands, paying us that first sowing and assisting us with all the necessities of livelihood to the harvesting of the first crop from which time we will begin to subsist on our own and contribute to Your Majesty that portion which is convenient to our situation to repay the cost of our travel and maintenance keeping for ourselves, our heirs and successors, the possession and perpetual ownership of the house, lands and live stock which will be assigned to us with all the other things we acquire and will acquire in said town.

All of which obliges us to what is here mutually and reciprocally contained and each one will comply with the correspondent part and for that reason we sign this duplicate contract in the city of Malaga on March 10, 1778, the witnesses being Don Joaquin Pizarro, Don Diego Terron and Joseph Montenegro. And because none of the interested parties know how to sign their names this was done for them by the witness Joseph Montenegro. Diego, Joaquin Pizarro, Don Joseph de Ortega y Monrroy.

As the clear reference and appearance of the cited agent to whom I relinquish and returned the original to the named Senor Don Joseph de Ortega that he sign here his receipt and at his petition give this to be sealed and signed in the city of Malaga on the 4th day of the month of June, 1778.

Luis Vidal

Don Joseph de Ortega y Monrroy
The scriveners of Our Lord the King. . . .

Miguel Romero.

I the undersigned scrivener of Our Lordship, the King, proclaim in all his kingdom and domains, resident of this city, certify and affirm that before me appeared Senor Don Joseph Ortega y Monrroy, priest of this same city, and deed whose contents are as follows:

Don Joseph de Ortega y Monrroy commissioned by His Majesty, may God guard him, for the enrollment of families from the kingdom of the Granada Coast to the towns of Louisiana, and Miguel Romero, native of Castuera, Bishopric of Badajoz, resident of the city of Malaga in the parish of the Holy Martyrs, forty years old, of the farming class. We say and contract, I the second, who am to pass in my person, that of my wife Maria Grano, native of the city of Malaga, thirty years old and my children Joseph fourteen years, Juan four years and Antonio one year, to settle in said towns to which we all go conformed, free and voluntarily without other force, violence or promise, other than that of the shares made to us in the name of His Majesty for which we will be disposed and readily present ourselves in this city of Malaga to embark and make the voyage as soon as the said Senor Commissioner orders it who will pay the cost of our maintenance from the day we leave our homes, and freight transportation to our arrival in Louisiana and that in the same he will give us comfortable lodgings, build us a house, assign lands to us, provide us with live stock, utensils and implements for cultivating and labor on the lands, paying us the first sowing and assisting us with all the necessities of livelihood to the harvesting of the first crop from which time we will begin to subsist on our own and contribute to Your Majesty that portion which is convenient to our situation to repay the cost of our travel and maintenance keeping for ourselves, our heirs and successors, the possession and perpetual ownership of the house, lands and live stock which will be assigned to us with all the other things we acquire and will acquire in said town.

All of which obliges us to what is here mutually and reciprocally contained and each one will comply with the correspondent part and for that reason we sign this duplicate contract in the city of Malaga on May 12, 1778 the witnesses being Don Joaquin Pizarro, Don Joseph Montenegro and Don Rafael de Rute. And because none of the interested persons know how to sign their names this was done for them by the witness Joseph Montenegro, Joaquin Pizarro, Rafael de Rute y Quevedo, Don Joseph de Ortega y Monrroy.

As the clear reference and appearance of the cited agent to whom I relinquish and returned the original to the named Senor Don Joseph de Ortega that he sign here his receipt and at his petition give this to be sealed and signed in the city of Malaga on the 4th day of the month of June, 1778.

Luis Vidal

Don Joseph Ortega y Monrroy
    The scriveners of Our Lord the King. . . .

Juan Solano.

I the undersigned scrivener of Our Lordship, the King, proclaim in all his kingdom and domains, resident of this city, certify and affirm that before me appeared Senor Don Joseph Ortega y Monrroy, priest of this city, the deed whose contents are as follows:

Don Joseph de Ortega y Monrroy commissioned by His

Majesty, may God guard him, for the enrollment of families from the kingdom of the Granada Coast to the towns of Louisiana, and Juan Solano, native of Alhaurin el Grande, resident of the city of Malaga in the parish of St. James, fifty-five years old widower of the farming class, we say and contract, I the second who is to pass in my person, that of my daughter Isabel Solano, married to Felix Garcia, native of Granada, thirty years of age and my grandsons, Joseph six years old and Felix two years old to settle in said towns to which all go conformed, free and voluntarily without other force, violence or promise than that of the shares made to us in the name of His Majesty for which we will be disposed and readily present ourselves in this city of Malaga to embark and make the voyage as soon as the said Senor Commissioner orders it who will pay the cost of our maintenance from the day we leave our homes, and freight transportation to our arrival in Louisiana and that in the same he will give us comfortable lodgings, build us a house, assign lands to us, provide us with live stock, utensils and implements for cultivating and labor on the lands, paying us the first sowing and assisting us with all the necessities of livelihood to the harvesting of the first crop from which time we will begin to subsist on our own and contribute to Your Majesty that portion which is convenient to our situation to repay the cost of our travel and maintenance keeping for ourselves, our heirs and successors, the possession and perpetual ownership of the house, lands and live stock which will be assigned to us with all the other things we acquire and will acquire in said town.

All of which obliges us to what is here mutually and reciprocally contained and each one will comply with the correspondent part and for that reason we sign this duplicate contract in the city of Malaga on May 12, 1778, the witnesses being Don Joaquin Pizarro, Don Rafael de Rute and Don Joseph Montenegro and because none of the interested persons could sign their names this was done for them by the witness Rafael de Rute y Quevedo. Joaquin Pizarro, Joseph Montenegro, Don Joseph de Ortega y Monrroy.

As the clear reference and appearance of the cited agent to whom I relinquish and returned the original to the named Senor Don Joseph de Ortega that he sign here his receipt and at his

petition give this to be sealed and signed in the city of Malaga
on the 4th day of the month of June, 1778.

Luis Vidal

Don Joseph de Ortega y Monrroy
The scriveners of Our Lord the King. . . .

Bernardo de Puentes.

I the undersigned scrivener of Our Lordship, the King, proclaim and affirm that before me appeared Senor Don Joseph
Ortega y Monrroy, priest of this same city, the deed whose
contents are as follows:

Don Joseph de Ortega y Monrroy commissioned by His
Majesty, may God guard him, for the enrollment of families
from the kingdom of the Granada Coast to the towns of Louisiana, and Bernardo de Puentes, native and resident of the town
of Macharavialla, thirty-one years old of the farming class, we
say and contract, I the second who am to pass in person, that
of my wife Ana Barreso, native of Algeciras, twenty-eight years
old and my daughter Maria, two years old to settle in said towns
to which we all go conformed, free and voluntarily without other
force, violence or promise than that of the shares made to us in
the name of His Majesty, for which we will be disposed and
readily present ourselves in the city of Malaga to embark and
make this voyage as soon as the said Senor Commissioner orders
it who will pay the cost of our maintenance from the day we
leave our homes, and freight transportation to our arrival in
Louisiana and that in the same he will give us comfortable
lodging, build us a house, assign lands to us, provide us with
live stock, utensils and implements for cultivating and labor
on the lands, paying us the first sowing and assisting us with
all the necessities of livelihood to the harvesting of the first
crop from which time we will begin to subsist on our own and
contribute to Your Majesty that portion which is convenient to
our situation to repay the cost of our travel and maintenance
keeping ourselves, our heirs and successors, the possession and
perpetual ownership of the house, lands and live stock which
will be assigned to us with all the other things we acquire and
will acquire in said town.

All of which obliges us to what is here mutually and reciprocally contained and each one will comply with the correspondent part and for that reason we sign this duplicate contract in the city of Malaga on May 15, 1778, the witnesses being Don Antonio Soler, Don Joaquin Pizarro, and Don Joseph Montenegro and signed for all his family Bernardo de Puentes. Antonio Soler, Joaquin Pizarro, Joseph Montenegro, Don Joseph de Ortega y Monrroy.

As the clear reference and appearance of the cited agent to whom I relinquish and returned the original to the named Senor Don Joseph de Ortega that he sign here his receipt and at his petition give this to be sealed and signed in the city of Malaga on the 4th day of the month of June, 1778.

Luis Vidal
Don Joseph de Ortega y Monrroy
The scriveners of Our Lord the King. . . .

Legajo no. 600

10.

My dear Sir;

I have received your Lordship's letter of the 12th of this month and as a consequence I have started to close all the business in conformity to Your Lordship's orders and to arrange everything to go up as quickly as possible.

The various items which Your Lordship has adverted to in the notice dated the 8th of this month I had the honor to pass on to Your Lordship and does not seem to have any connection with the main object of my commission, I intend if Your Lordship approves to give something to the Indian nation of Chetis Machas, if I should settle on the outskirts of the huts which they have along the Teche, as by route of the outskirts so that they will not look with sorrow before, but with pleasure to the settlement of these families on ground they occupy although useless as to cultivation and that these same Indians will provide me with the abundance necessary of game and fish (in which they occupy themselves) for the maintenance of these families. Also if Your Lordship approves I intend to give small gifts in Your Lordship's name as Governor General of this province and as representive of the sovereignty to the chiefs of the small nations of the Atacapas who are found in these outskirts and make them grateful so that they will not injure and follow the example of the great Atacapas, who with much reason is attributed the mistreatment committed against Don Luis Andry, which gifts I believe necessary, but I will not make them without all possible economy and giving Your Lordship punctual notice of everything.

With this I have taken the liberty to enclose to Your Lordship notice of the Malagan families who came on this occasion with me and of others who remain here for reasons I have mentioned and will give in detail in the margin of each family.

Other persons have come to me but so as not to take many people on this first trip, perceiving the hard season and no lodging I will encounter there suddenly it seems to me more proper (excepting the dictate of Your Lordship) not to take more people now but those on the enclosed detailed report with the exception of M. Penalver a licensed soldier who wishes to settle himself and who can be useful to me by his honorable way of thinking.

May God Our Lord keep Your Lordship for many years. New Orleans and January 14, 1779.

I kiss Your Lordship's hand. Your most attentive and obedient servant.

Francisco Bouligny (seal)

Senor Don Bernardo de Galbez.

Notice of the Malagan families who go with me on this occasion to settle themselves on the Teche on the partition of the Atacapas in comformity to the orders of Senor Don Bernardo de Galbez, Governor General of this province, and of the detailed names and ages of each individual.

1st Family

Miguel Romero age	35	years
Maria Grano his wife age	40	"
Josef Romero his son	13	"
Juan Romero his son age	3	"
Antonio Romero his son age	1	"

2nd Family

Theresa Gomez widow age	46	"
Antonio Villatoro her son	21	"

Maria Villatoro her daughter   13 years
Juana Villatoro her daughter   11 "
3rd Family
Bernardo de Aponte age
Ana Varroso his wife   25 "
4th Family
Francisco Balderas single   28 "
5th Family
Joseph Lagos single   50 "
6th Family
Francisco Segura single   18 "
7th Family
Josef de Porras single   28 "
8th Family
Francisco Ortiz age   33 "
Francisca Blanco his wife   32 "
Catalina Ortiz his daughter   9 "
Juan Ortiz his son   5 "
Ana Ortiz his daughter   1 "
which eight families number twenty persons.

New Orleans, January 14, 1779.

                     Francisco Bouligny (seal)

Note: Miguel Penalver, licensed soldier of this battalion, age 55 years goes also on this occasion.

                     Francisco Bouligny (seal)

Notice of the Malagan families who remain here for the reasons detailed in the margin of each one and who can go up when their health and circumstances permit and the Governor General of this province finds it agreeable.

First

Luis Molina, overseer and young single man   24 years

This young man has lost his father and brother who came as overseers and were intelligent countrymen. He finds himself forelorn and little fit for the toils of the field for this motive and because of his

Oil Derrick, Iberia Parish.

Inside Morton Salt Mine at Week's Island. (Photo by Kennametal, Inc.)

Floods in the Teche country, Louisiana. A sketch by J. O. Davidson which appeared in Harper's Weekly, March 29, 1891. (From the collection of Leonard V. Huber.)

honesty I think he is deserving and who begs Your Lordship some concession from the King.

2nd Family

Juan Lopez	40	years
Maria Ruiz his wife	35	"
Juana Fernandez his mother-in-law	55	"
Feliz Ruiz her son	14	"
Francisca Ruiz her daughter	12	"
Josefa Ruiz her daughter	9	"
Rafael Ruiz her son	2	"

The wife is on the verge of giving delivery.

3rd Family

Juan Garrido	50	"
Inez Maldonado	37	"
Catalina Villalba	11	"
Juan Garrido	3	"

This woman also is on the verge of delivery.

4th Family

Lorenza Mancebo widow	46	"
Ana Morena her daughter	18	"
Josefa Morena her daughter	14	"
Francisco Morena her son	12	"
Maria Moreno her daughter	10	"
Fernando Moreno her son	8	"

. .
There is no man in this family able to work and because of sex and ages in no condition to go up. Because of her situation she is deserving of the help and patronage of Your Lordship f r o m the King.

5th Family

Pedro Guerrero	22	"
Roza de Cuevas his wife	16	"

This man is a barber and can go up on the second trip if you approve or he can remain

Maria Guerrero his daughter	2 years	

here to w o r k as a barber where he can more easily earn his living and not be a burden to the interests of the King.

6th Family

Juan Migues	30	"
Salvadora de Quero his wife	27	"
Salvador his son	3	"

The woman of this family is sick and in no condition to undertake the trip at this time.

7th Family

Josef Artacho	38	"
Francisca Villegas his wife	36	"
Gregorio his son	15	"
Maria his daughter	9	"
Christoval his son	4	"

The husband of this woman is sick with tertian fever. He can go up on the second trip.

8th Family

Feliz Martinez	25	"
Agustin Solano his wife	22	"
Juan Solano her father	60	"
Josef Martinez his son	8	"

The woman is on the verge of delivery.

9th Family

Gonzales de Prados	38	"
Theresa Gusman his wife	38	"
Manuel le Prados	17	"
Maria de Prados	15	"
Theresa de Prados	6	"
Gertrudes de Prados	13	"

This woman also is on the verge of delivery.

10th Family

Josef de Lagos	38	"
Juana Morena	33	"
Maria de Lagos	16	"
Nicolas Minos	16	"

This family has a great dislike to going up. The woman particularly alleges that she knows nothing a b o u t the

Salvador de Lagos	3 years	fields and that she is in a position to earn her living by sewing. If you approve she can go up on the second trip or separate herself from the town.
11th Family		
Juan Gonzales	17 "	This youth knows nothing of field work. He is practicing in the hospital to be a Practitioner. He can go up on the second trip or work in the hospital if Your Lordship finds that agreeable.
Rita Villatoro	16 "	

New Orleans, January 14, 1779.

Francisco Bouligny (seal)

Legajo no. 2358

20.

My dear Sir;

I convey to Your Lordships that about the 11th of this month we entered the Teche River having delayed the trip because we found all the bayous which lead to the lake closed and it was necessary to reenter the Chafalaya to cross this lake.

On the 12th we met Mr. Declouet who came behind me offering to help me in all, after having an ample conference about all the advantages and inconveniences which this country presents I noticed in this same immediate meeting the country of the Chetis Machas whose chief is Soulis Rouge. I have determined to settle here because it is near the exit to the sea where one can go in two days all assure me, by the nearness of a port, one quarter league to the lake, the closest place to the cypress trees for the construction of the houses, the goodness of the soil and of the vast pastures does not leave many inconveniences because of the long distance I am from the center of the Atacapas and of Mr. Declouet. I am a day's walk from here but I have preferred this site because I have not yet found any other establishment. Excepting that of two free Negroes, one already condemned by Mr. Declouet to leave here and the other who complies well for taking the concession which awaits Your Lordship in the part farther down the Teche; Mr. Declouet has told me about other grants which he awaits from Your Lordship but no one having formed an establishment no one could reverse those same grants in Falsa Punta or another site without causing great prejudice leaving to all in common the cypress as is my desire and which principal goal I had when asking for these grants in the day when the town comes which will be started here and the fond hope of finding a good pass to the sea, all are ambitious for grants with the desire of gaining them, than cultivating them.

Regarding the Indians who ceded to me two cabins and a small fence, I gave them fifteen pesos in money and a present of about a hundred pesos, also satisfying as laborers fourteen Indians who have given me the chief to help me remount the barges through Plaquemine to the river.

The families who came with me are very happy and a soldier, who came with the skill of oarsman called Gabriel, also asked me to settle with them under this occasion to establish themselves on a small island and leave later if Your Lordship found it agreeable.

I propose to assign to each six arpents of ground in front of the river on the right side mounting the Teche for cultivation and six on the left side where I will found the place which ground will remain a common pasture for the grazing of all the animals with the liberty for each to make a fence around the piece of land that belongs to each if they wish to cultivate it.

I will mark the place in one hundred plots but will not settle more than twenty-five families on its leaving the other plots for grants to those who wish to settle on them like Mercaderes the officials and assigning them by royalty a large space for the needs the future might offer.

The families are happy with the plot of ground I have assigned them and as all will be treated equally there will be no reason for complaints or envies notwithstanding economizing as much as I can see that the cost is high and to make these men in charge pay the expenses would be a set back and impossible to make headway with this enterprise for this reason I hope Your Lordship's kind heart will be moved to secure some benefice of the Sovereign for them.

Mr. Pollock has written to beg me to stop at his place when we go down in the barges to pick up the tobacco he has made. I have adhered to it because I do not find it inconvenient to ask the overseer to be responsible to Mr. Pollock for the setback this loading of the tobacco would cause.

I wish the most perfect health for Your Lordship and may God our Lord, keep you for many years. New Iberia, February 18, 1779.

I kiss Your Lordship's hand. Your most attentive and obedient servant.

Francisco Bouligny

Senor Don Bernardo de Galbez.

Legajo no. 600

22.

I send to Your Lordship on this occasion four Malagan families who number twenty-four persons whose sex and ages Your Lordship will be informed of on the enclosed list.

Las *Berges* which will take them are in charge of Gregorio Bo and Miguel Rodriguez with ten oarsmen each. These go for an agreement of five and one-half bits[3] a day with the condition that they are to maintain to their account and to that of their patrons at seven and one-half bits.

So that they can get their provisions I have put at the disposal of Gregorio Bo one hundred forty pesos which he has received and is recorded in the enclosed document and it will give Your Lordship an account of what I have provided to each oarsman in order that with this knowledge you can decide the amount and satisfy them. The rest should be given in payments beginning March 3.

From the enclosed abstract Your Lordship will be informed of what has been provided here to the families which amount each one has listed in his note book.

Your Lordship will send a receipt to Don Juan Bentura

---

[3]A *real* (bit) is equal to twelve and one-half cents. Two reales are equal to twenty-five cents or two bits, an expression which was in common usage in this area at one time.

Morales for the 7,398 reales which value the said abstract amount to including the one hundred forty pesos provided to the patron so that Your Lordship can be informed of the corresponding general account and these expenses I will give in detail in the report of the others occasioned by this establishment in your care.

The named patron is in charge of the utilities which the enclosed note manifests for the preparation of the Berches. May Our Lord keep Your Lordship many years. New Orleans, March 4, 1779.

Senor Don Francisco Bouligny.

Report of the four Malagan families who went up with Don Francisco Bouligny to settle on the Teche in the new town of New Iberia.

1st Family
Gonzalo de Prados.......... 38 years
Teresa Guzman .... 38 "
Manuel de Prados........... 17 "
Maria de Prados............ 15 "
Gertrudis de Prados........ 13 "
Teresa de Prados........... 6 "
An infant .... 1 month

2nd Family
Juan Lopez .... 40 "
Maria Ruiz his wife......... 35 "
Juana Fernandez
    his mother-in-law .... 55 "
Feliz Ruiz .... 14 "
Francisca Ruiz .... 12 "
Josefa Ruiz .... 9 "
Rafael Ruiz .... 2 "

3rd Family
Juan Garrido .... 50 "
Inez Maldonado .... 37 "
Catalina Villalba daughter .... 11 "
Juan Garrido .... 3 "
An Infant ....1½ months

4th Family

Josef Artacho .... 38 Years
Francisca Villegas .... 36 "
Maria .... 9 "
Christoval .... 4 "
New Orleans, March 4, 1779.

23.

Legajo no. 2,358

My dear Sir;

With the patron who returned the barge I had the honor to communicate to Your Lordship my arrival at Chetis Machas whose beautiful location and excellent quality of soils appears to me to be very favorable for the establishment of this town as much for cultivation as for the raising of all kinds of animals. To my judgment it would be difficult to find another site with as many advantages and even though in this distance of twelve leagues there are sections of woods one can settle on six arpents along both banks of the Teche about two hundred families with much space and they can begin to cultivate without cutting one single tree more than twenty-four thousand arpents leaving a vast and immense pasture where they can graze and raise a credible number of animals.

At an equal distance of twelve leagues with little difference there is from here to the presbytery where Mr. Declouet lives always following the Teche in this same distance is already occupied by thirty-five or forty proprietors who could raise an equal number of animals but cultivation would be very reduced and in proportion to the small number of hands they could employ but with regard to the extension of the cultivatable fields it is without comparison greater in the other part than here.

In the haste to attend and continually work in order to temporarily shelter all from the inclemencies of the weather if I had not occupied Mr. Flamand and Mr. Henderson I would have sent to Your Lordship with this occasion a rigid plan of what each has done since his entrance from Plaquemine to here, which plans if they do not have the exactitude regarding distance since the one has been made by estimate and the other with the clock in the hand no doubt I could give Your Lordship a complete knowledge of the immensity of these lakes and canals which the delta of this Mississippi River has formed for the Chafalaya in the twenety-five or thirty leagues which could be the distance from here to the river.

Mr. Coleta previously settled in this same place has told me that the gulf coast runs about parallel with the Teche and is not far from here about three or four leagues to the southwest but can only be reached by a firm foot and by a tongue of ground which is about three or four leagues farther down from here and which nevertheless is all low land and impassable.

Several persons have assured me that one can go from here by Barataria to my habitation in three or four days going by bayous and very navigable canals without going to the sea and without strong currents either going or coming which would be of the greatest advantage in establishing a quick communication and much less costly than by Chafalaya and Plaquemine. I have sent word to a hunter of Opelousas named Bartelimi whom they say frequently makes this trip and as soon as Mr. Flamand arrives I will send him with him to look over and mark well the route and all on behalf of Your Lordship.

Clavert's embarkation which from Barataria Lake went to the sea by the Big River where this Teche empties and went farther up on this same about seven or eight leagues.

The prosperity and growth of this new town and of the old inhabitants of Opelousas, Vermilion and Atacapas depends upon having an easy exit for the marketing of their produce and in order to encourage the businessmen to come seeking and providing these farmers with whatever they might need with which important object I will occupy myself and communicate to Your Lordship all the discoveries that can be made.

A few days after my arrival I sowed the hemp, the wheat and the barley which Your Lordship gave me. The last two have sprouted because without doubt the seed was old but many here have made this experience and assure me these plants do well. The Malagans base their hopes on the wheat in preference to all the others because of the experience they have had with this cultivation. If Your Lordship receives some from Spain I deserve that Your Lordship reserve a part for me to distribute to these families because that which I brought is very little.

If Your Lordship would send me here the seeds I would place and plant them in the site where could be produced the hemp and the flax this coming year. If they arrive in September or October of this year and the hemp seed is fresh I will take care of this task and if all is favorable as I hope I will call attention to all the others so that they can be encouraged to this important cultivation at whose development it will contribute greatly if the expense of these first years be paid by Your Magd. all the produce they raise fixing a price somewhat profitable, which Your Lordship can if you find it convenient consult the higher authority about it.

Until now the families here have subsisted but now they each have a cabin which I helped them to make with the aid of the Negroes, made of board covered with dirt and palmetto. They are moving on the bare ground and when it is ready I will have given to them food until the end of September and whatever else you judge necessary for your development which expenses together with those which I made until now I will send to Your Lordship in detail as soon as I am a little less occupied.

I have bought thirty-two pair of oxen, ten untrained and twenty-two trained these at forty to forty-five pesos a pair and the others at thirty; twenty cows at fifteen pesos each, twelve horses at twenty-five pesos, six mares at fourteen pesos and one portion of pigs and chickens which price with the expenses they made, I will add to the particular account of the families to which they were distributed making the oxen work in the meantime plowing the ground and extracting the timber from the cypress grove.

Mr. Declouet is the one who bought all these animals for me and has assured me they could not have been better placed but for the sale it would be more advantageous to buy a dairy for about five hundred to a thousand reses and from which Your Lordship could also get the animals necessary for the other establishments chosen but I will not decide without your approbation and the good pleasure of Your Lordship although you did not write to tell me at the price of the cattle in this case so as to advise Your Lordship but I did not get an answer.

As the grass here is very thick and a single pair of oxen which I intend to give each family is not enough to open the prairie I make them each plow eight or ten arpents of ground which will give them much relief and they can raise their produce this year in corn, rice and maybe a little tobacco.

I have warned Mr. Declouet if he had any poor families in Opelousas and Atacapas who were farmers that he would send them to me and I would place them like the others in conformity to the wishes of Your Lordship.

I met four German families when I first crossed the Big River and they were in the greatest misery and unhappiness so I told them to come here and settle with the others.

Also of the Negroes whom I prepared for Your Lordship before leaving the city I leased from Mr. Arnoul one named Bastien whom I have kept here and who serves me as foreman of the *Bato* to bring back and forth the necessities from Atacapas.

Also before I left the city I made a deal with Dublin a professional blacksmith and a good man to come with me to work in all that might be necessary for forty pesos a month and his rations. He is indispensible to me because it is impossible to use many of the implements without tempering them.

The Malagans have asked me with eagerness for plows like those used in Spain if there are any in the warehouses I will be grateful if Your Lordship would send them to me and from this same model I will have the blacksmith make some for all but since they can manage with it once the prairie is open with only one pair of oxen it would be for those here who need at least three pairs.

The labor which the Negroes have done until the present has helped the families to make themselves a cabin on the property of each one, two warehouses for provisions covered with palmetto, a cabin covered with *pieux* for Mr. Flamand and for Don Juan Tala, one for Mr. Henderson, one for the Blacksmith and in this the blacksmith shop, another for the soldiers. Now there are plowed about twelve or fifteen arpents of ground for the families, fifty pieces of cypress of eighteen feet which have been made in the cypress mill, a large coal oven, two fences one on each side to enclose the animals and a pile of wood to make a bridge and be able to conveniently cross the animals over the two hundred forty foot wide Teche. Messrs. Flamand and Henderson have worked hard and zealously but I do not believe that in the summer they will be able to stand such strenuous fatigue so when the house-building begins I plan to have an intelligent Acadian man on their construction so he can help them and they can work at the sedentary work which is necessary such as the plan of the place of every house and of all the Teche up to here which I wish to send Your Lordship as soon as possible.

I have over the crossway, Escanimon a chief of a small nation of the Atacapas living in Vermilion with twenty-five persons counting men, women and children, another chief named Cahauche with fifteen men living over the *Carcacionx*, another named Mamo with twenty men living at a small *arrojo* in the middle of Opelousas. A few days ago Mementao another chief of the Atacapas with thirty men was here. None of them brought me any news of Andry. Mementao only brought me two little pieces of paper, one with the name of Andry written in pencil in his own handwriting and on the other Millet which papers were given to two Indians of his nation whom he met at the sea shore. Escaminonx has told me he sent three men to a place, Friend of the Curcapas, to acquire all notices possible for its success and that they will come to tell me about it. He has told me that his nation is at war with the Carcapas and that this nation is divided into five settlements, three of them weak and two very strong which are on an isle which is the Bay of San Bernardo and that they come to solid ground by foot with the water coming only as high as their knees or half thigh. As to the other questions I asked I could learn nothing more, so to get rid of them a present which includes the one Mementao brought amounting to one hundred fifty pesos including the food and I have told them that I would absolutely not give them anything more unless they brought me personal information about all that happened to Don Luis Andry.

The desire and anxiety to see everything here a little better arranged has not given me time to go to Atacapas and Opelousas but in brief I plan to go if there are any disagreements and arguments and I plan to settle all the best way possible.

I beg Your Lordship to believe that my desire, my only desire, is not only to obey in all, and as I should, all the orders of Your Lordship but also to give Your Lordship proofs of the great delight in which I will fulfill the least wish of Your Lordship and of the particular affection that I profess and will eternally profess to you personally whose life I beg of God to preserve for many years.

New Iberia, March 17, 1779. I kiss Your Lordship's hand I assure you I am your Lordship's most attentive servant and subject.

Francisco Bouligny (seal)
Senor Don Bernardo de Galbez.

Legajo no. 600

40.

IIerein are enclosed to Your Lordship the testamonial copies of the contracts made in Malaga by the farmers Juan Migues, Francisco Ortiz, Antonio Villatoro, Miguel Romero, Bernardo de Puentes, Juan Lopez, Josef de Artacho, Gonzalo de Prados, Juan Garrido and Julian de Aguilar who live in this settlement so that Your Lordship can attend to the termination of what was stipulated in them making a separate account of the amount taken in Spain for their maintenance. Upon receiving it Your Lordship will inform me.

May God keep you for many years. New Orleans, June 7, 1779. Bernardo de Galvez. Senior Don Francisco Bouligny.

Legajo no. 2358

1.

Report of all the provisions made to the family of Antonio Villatoro, composed of four persons, he, his mother and two brothers from January 28 of the present year when they left New Orleans to the present day.

	Reales	Maravedizes
63 days of ration for 4 individuals from January 28 to March 31 of meat, bacon, bread and miscellaneous are rations at 2½ bits (37½¢) each	630.	
Meat from April 1 to May 16, 179 pounds		

at 4s *tornezes* per pound	57.	----11
6 cans of lard	24.	
1 barrel of rice	40.	
½ barrel of peas	12.	
12 chickens	24.	
5 barrels of potatoes	30.	
3 pounds of butter	9.	
In the month of April	8.	
Same for May	10.	
For lard until the end of September	40.	
1 mule which Mr. Yudiz bought	96.	
1 horse	200.	
2 cows	240.	
Tobacco	10.	
On other occasion	24.	
1 chair	24.	
Soap	4.	
	1,476.	----11

Importan the expenses occasioned by this family to the present 1,476 reales 11 maravedizes to which account ought to be added the effects that I have made from the warehouse of the King, detailed in the enclosed report and the fresh meat provided him twice a week since May 16 which are 12 pounds each time at 4s torneces.

New Iberia, June 26, 1779
Francisco Bouligny.

2.

Notice of the effects that by the order of Senor Don Francisco Bouligny *theniente* of the Governor of this province and commissioned to form New Iberia I have provided to the family of Antonio Villatoro from the royal warehouse which in this town is in my care.

Pesos.-Reales.-Marv.

For a shot gun	6.		
2 gunpowder		7	14
4 bird shot	1.		

Item			
2 bullets		4	
18 small bullets			17
2 hoes or spades	3.		
1 hand saw	2.	4	
1 sickle		6	
2 hand axes	1.	4	
2 axes	4.		
3 wedges	3.	6	
46 *varas de coleta* at 3 reales ½	20.	1	
12 pounds of nails	3.		
2 measures 1 of 7 points,			
1 of 12 at 2 rs. a point	4.	6	
1 skillet	1.	6	
1 small auger or drill		1	17
1 measuring line		4	
11 soap	2.	6	
1 half-ax	1.	2	
5 pairs of shoes	10.		
2 ordinary knives		1	12
2 carpenter's *suelas*	4.		
3 chisels	1.	4	
2 large drills	2.	4	
2 padlocks	3.		
1 more sickle		6	
2 files	1.	2	22
16 more *varas coleta*	8.		
1 measure of 4 points	1.		
2½ pieces of calico	15		
3 jackets of *coleta*	3.	3	
1½ pieces of cord for tobacco	3.		
1 frog thread	1.		
1 barrel of flour	20.		
another of the same	22.		
2 barrels of flour divided among three			
families, 1 for 25 pecos the other for 22.	15.	5	17
50 *haujas*		2	
	170	6	31

Which amount is one thousand three hundred seventy-six reales and thirty-one maravediz. New Iberia, June 22, 1779.

Juan Tala (seal)

Francisco Bouligny (seal)

3.

Notice and provincial memorandum for the intelligence of Senor Don Bernardo de Galvez, Governor General of this Province, of the expenses occasioned in the establishment of New Iberia and distribution of the twelve thousand pesos which I have received in cash.

	(quantity)	(total received)
Supplied by Pecalvert		12,000 pesos
To the account of the thirty-five Negroes that I have here	1,000	
Ditto supplied to the same on various occasions	160	
For the supplements given to the family of Antonio Villatoro according to the detailed paper enclosed no. 1 without including the effects of the warehouse	179-6-11	
Ditto for Juan Migues	157- -17	
Ditto for Francisco Hortiz	192-7-	
Ditto for Francisco Segura	102- - 8	
Ditto for Miguel Romeo	203-5	
Ditto for Josef Porras	76-6- 8	
Ditto for Francisco Banderas	78-5- 8	
Ditto for Bernardo de Puentes	150-	
Ditto for Gonzalo de Prados	138-5-14	
Ditto for Juan Lopez	144-7-16	
Ditto for Josef Artacho	130- -17	
Ditto for Juan Garrido	113-7-17	
Ditto for Julian Aguilar	82-1	
For Rafael Bidal	105-1-	
For M. La Coterai	129- -25	
For Josef Fernandez	53-3-17	
For Gabriel Lopez	68-7-17	
For Jayme Narpar	40-1	

For Adan Carlos 41-2
For Juan Henrrique............. 40-1
For Mathias Grim 23-4
For Luis Boute 27-7
For various subjects sent to Opelousas
   before I left New Orleans.
To Henrrique Pumphri 10-7- 5
To Gabriel Martin 10-7- 5
To Zaquerias Martin 10-7- 5
To Gideon Thomas 10-7- 5
To Roberto Roberts 10-7- 5
To Juan Livre 10-7- 5
To Samuel Sisd 10-7- 5
To Lucas Fort 34-2-17
To Thomas Par 10-4
To Lucas Garcia 16-5
To Eduart Former 17-5
To M. Jean Bte. Grevembert Flamand
   to his account of 60 pesos assigned
   him each month 375-
To M. Henderson the same 250-
To the warehouse guard Don Juan
   Tala to his account 100-
To Doblin, Master blacksmith 277-4
To M. Bervick to his good account .. 247-4
To the Indians in money and food on
   various occasions without includ-
   ing the present given in goods
   from the the warehouse 35-
Expenses caused by the master sailors
   and pilots of the first expedition of
   the three *Baloes* 511-3-17
The cited patrons were paid by means
   of my receipt for which reason I am
   not including the cost here
Liquid paid here to the patron
   D'Apena, 3rd payment 112-1
To the Acadians who plowed 20
   arpents of ground for the families 35-3-17

Spring Time in Bird City. Nest in front shows a pair of young American egrets.

Jungle Gardens at Avery Island, Louisiana.

To Stuar to his account of 20 pesos
a month for attending and watching
over the work of the Negroes in the
woods 15-
To Coleta for buying his land 400-
To Postillon to the good account of
the meat he supplied since May 16 180-
Daily pay supplied to the Corporal and
4 soldiers for the 5 months of February, March, April, May, June .. 205-
In M. Declouet's care for payment on
various expenses 130-
33 pairs of oxen in stock 1,202-
Paid to Pedro Brousart for conducting
these animals 53-
For a large pirogue purchased by
M. Coleta 60-
For 10 horses in stock 250-
For 26 sheep (male) in stock 65-
For 30 pigs bought at different prices
in stock 125-
For 10 pigs that M. Declouet sent me
in the old settlement and suffocated
on the way because of the excessive
heat 100-
For 180 pounds of candles which
expense was added to the account of
the warehouse 55-
For a *obtante* and a compass which
I bought from M. Pollock and which
note I left in town which cost if
I remember right 60-
For 500 pounds of powder which cost
is also added to the warehouse where
it is in stock 218-6
For 3 pairs of wheels and 1 cart
which I bought at the first settlement 34-
Ditto for 77 posts 38-4

For 100 barrels of corn for planting
and replacement 62-4
For a Devil's lock purchased for
M. Sacier 15-
For the trip of M. Fran. Flamand
to the city 16-
Money on hand 830-

                                 9,645-.........23
Something is lacking and this amount
I am charging to the hiring of the
Negroes who are in the care of M.
Flamand .... 2,354-7-........9

                                 12,000-
Notice.— In this last division there were various small expenses
of which it was not possible to keep note of all.
Another.—The 12,000 pesos which I ordered of Your Lordship
M. Maxant, the foreman receipted and received to the account of
the warehouse according to what the cited Maxant has produced.
Another.—The other receipts which I have given in addition to
this 24,000 pesos with entry for expenditure.

New Iberia, June 26, 1779.

Francisco Bouligny (seal)

Legajo no. 600
69.

To Senor Don Bernardo de Galbez, Knight of the distinguished
order of Charles III, Colonel of the Royal Army and Governor
and Intendant General of the Louisiana Province. — on the
River.—

My dear Sir;

I am enclosing to Your Lordship a list of the people I brought
with me; the desire to sacrifice my life for my King and to prove
to Your Lordship my personal affection and my inclination is the
agent which moves me; I have come here with Mr. Delcouet and
our trip was most united and friendly, like him I await the
orders of Your Lordship and will execute it with the greatest

fervor for all my satisfaction is in that. I pray that God will keep you for many years. From Casa Champaña, September 3, 1779.

I kiss Your Lordship's hand, your most devoted servant and subject.

Francisco Bouligny (seal)

Senor Don Bernardo de Galbez.

List of the people who went with me to New Iberia and arrived here following the military post of Monsieur Declouet

Soldiers

Thomas Aragon 2nd Commander of the 8
Antonio Dominguez soldier of the 4th
Juan Lazaro same of the 3rd
Pedro Ruis same of the 4th
Luis Marcos same of the 5th 5

Licensed Soldiers

Gabriel Lopez licensed grenadier
Pedro Blacer soldier of the 4th same 2

Desertors

Antonio Peña desertor *presentado*
Antonio Toisa *precidario* and desertor *presentado* 2

Farmers

Francisco Segura Malagan farmer unmarried
Josef de Porras farmer same 2

Militia

Noel Doublin Master Blacksmith and Militia-man in
    Monsieur Belleille's company 1

Americans

Thomas Beard American
Juan Abseher same 2

Volunteers and employed in New Iberia

Don Juan de Tala
Don Luis Loyssel 2
                                                    ———
                                                     16

That which makes 16 persons all in state of activity and full of zeal.

The four soldiers and the corporal have armament the others

have some guns of trade but without adequate bullets and without any white arms.

List and state of the 25 Negroes that I brought with me in this expedition.

20	Creoles		
	Zefir	40 years—axes	
	Lo. Evelle	30	1
	Claudio	24	1
	Antonio	24	
	Franco Augustin	18	
	Inacio	28	1
	Zaxier	25	
	Loullo	22	1
	Grand Luis	30	1
	Juan Bautista	18	1
	Juan	22	1
	L'Grillade	40	
	Josef Dutor	30	1
	Agustin	35	1
	Yorck	28	
	Soliman	21	
	Jacobo	40	
	Cezar	38	1
	Josef Religiosso	20	
	Alexi	24	1
4	Rough		
	Felemaque	25	1
	Bte. Nago	25	
	Vicente Nago	25	1
	Baltazar	25	
			——
			13

The first twenty-one Negroes are creoles and good marksmen the last four use the ax well.

Plaquemine, Casa de Champaña, 2 o'clock in the afternoon, September 3, 1779.

Francisco Bouligny (seal)

So as not to delay the mail which Mr. Declouet will dispatch I did not reveal the mistake there is in this statement of one Negro.

Franco Bouligny

Legajo no. 600

72.

My dear Sir;

In consequence of the information which Your Lordship asked of me the 26th of this month to determine at my last request to know how much more I could spend to finish the establishment of these families, how long it would take or would be necessary and by what means I intend to avail myself in order to verify it with the greatest promptitude: equally attending to the present happenings of this colony since the 1st of September and of the great advantages offered by the immense and rich lands conquered by Your Lordship from Manchak to the *Oyo* whose coast faces ours, the oldest and richest establishment presents great comfort for the new towns because of the nearness to this capital and benefits by being on the same side of the river. With attention to all I will expound to Your Lordship the plan of operation which seems to me to be relatively the most convenient to the formation of New Iberia and the quick establishment of the families Your Lordship has placed in my care; understanding especially the points over which Your Lordship asked me to be informed as much as possible and over which plan subject in all to the decision and superior light of Your Lordship, I await the approbation or orders which Your Lordship finds convenient to give me those which serve the North and destroy the perplexity or pain which will remain although my good will does not choose the better part.

It is impossible to fix with certainty the possible cost of concluding the establishment of these families ignoring the produce that I left to them, being my intention if Your Lordship wills it well, to raise the allotments of corn and rice that I have let them produce or in money if this were not sufficient so that each family should have its subsistence for the coming year and for the proper allotments: also it seems to me better to give them in money the cost of the house rather than have them made, making

— 149 —

them build it themselves and I think it would be advantageous to adhear to it, but not offering the same situation as the first they were in, the gathering of these and the cypress lumber would be very costly to build each one a house with tenant Negroes or by the enterprise of the inhabitants of which some came to me to ask for five hnndred pesos to build one just like the one I had made twenty-eight feet long, the other dimensions I believe I have already given Your Lordship some time past and which I do not have here with me. This higher price inclines me to think it would be better to give each family according to number of individuals in the family, two or three hundred pesos with which they could buy the kind of house the Acadians want to sell them, desirous to wander in the distance because of the growing number of animals which they now have and the others ask a concession for the same which is vacant and more comfortable and where with this money and assistance they themselves could form their settlement a method which seems to me to be the quickest and simplest and which to my understanding amply fulfills Your Majesty's contract.

The Negroes will be occupied until next January 17 which terminates the contract which their bosses made in helping the families harvest their produce, transporting them to their habitations, picking up the lumber cut in the first establishment and taking it to New Iberia and building in the town some houses for the official men such as the carpenters, the blacksmith, shoemaker and especially one for the surgeon whose mansion there as the center of the Atacapas will enable him to help these families in whatever part he finds them, I will put all my effort that on the cited day of January 17 all will be exactly concluded and marked out the town into one hundred plots, the vacant lots can be granted to those who wish to establish themselves in it.

Concerning the warehouse and my living quarters which together form one respectable building as it will be a little away from the town and can be made into a habitation of ten or twelve arpents in front on the Bayou Teche with the same fence which it had when the ground was bought from Coleta and could serve for lodging of the commandant of this district or it could be sold at a public sale and give some credit to compensate Your Majesty for the expense of building it. The cypress lumber which was cut in the first establishment with the intention of building a church will serve those who can extract it without costing much for the buildings which I have mentioned for houses for the official. It does not seem to me a convenient time now to build a church here on account of the small number of subjects in this town especially since there is one three leagues from here where they can go to hear mass provided that Your Lordship sends a priest which seems to me very appropriate not only for these families but also for all the other inhabitants of this district which number has grown sufficiently and find many obstacles in going to find spiritual helps at Opelousas at a great distance and sometimes over dangerous roads.

The hiring of the seventy-five Negroes not counting two months of the twenty-four occupied in this project and whom I took with me to the Manchack expedition will amount to fifteen to sixteen thousand pesos a year of which I have turned over to the proprietors up to now only five thousand two hundred pesos. Before leaving there I left Mr. Boutet six hundred pesos to help the families during the month of October and part of November in which month they will reap their produce and I will suspend all aid excepting to the family of the deceased Ibañes for which I will procure assistance according to the events and in conformity as Your Lordship has given me orders. When the year ends I will discharge all the employees excepting the surgeon whom I will continue to occupy if Your Lordship finds it is agreeable to conclude the contract which I had the honor to communicate to Your Lordship for approval that your mansion there will be very useful not only for these families but also for all other inhabitants.

In the itemizing of all these expenses I will charge (always according to the dictates of Lour Lordship) to the particular account of each family only that which I entrusted to them in money or the value of their effects or collected animals and one hundred fifty pesos only to each family for the various tasks and assistance which the Negroes gave them by their labors charging all of the rest to extraordinary expenses since it would be impossible to satisfy without setting them back in their work.

It is true that the sum of 31,150 pesos which according to my receipts I have collected until the present forms an object of sufficient consideration, but the circumstances of the times, the high cost of everything, the costliness of communication, the flood which happened in the first place, the inseparable difficulties of the first steps of a double establishment has caused the cost to increase. The contract with these families in which Your Majesty was obliged to support and assist until the harvest of their first produce has obliged me from the beginning to propose to Your Lordship and take with me a number of Negroes assuring in the first year this harvest which was saved in spite of the great detriment which was caused by the flood and the advanced season at that time, saves Your Majesty many expenses which would have been indispensable to make with them in the next year.

Also I must make known to Your Lordship that of the named sum Mr. Maxant has on hand five thousand pesos and there in effect about three thousand which amount I cannot fix with certainty because I do not have here any of the documents relating to this; if Your Lordship finds it agreeable the first could be added to the account of that which Mr. Maxant provides for the other establishments and the rest or liquidate them there if they were not broken in their sale or return them here since all are effects of primary necessity in these actual circumstances.

With the orders which Your Lordship will find convenient to give me regarding these particulars, I will begin at once to put them into execution with all the animation and zeal there is in me.

May God, our Saviour, guard the important life of Your Lordship the many years I wish for you. New Orleans, October 28, 1779.

I kiss Your Lordship's hand your most attentive servant and obedient subject.

Francisco Bouligny (seal)
Senor Don Bernardo de Galbez.

Legajo no. 600
74.
My dear Sir;
As a result of Your Lordship's letter dated yesterday I cannot do less than tell Your Lordship that the subjects failed to

tell Your Lordship the truth when they informed Your Lordship that the inhabitants of the Atacapas are obliged to plant; Messrs. Borel and Flamand who are here and who had a part of the place plowed could inform Your Lordship of the method I used with it and with Messrs. De L'Houssaye and Boutet who also had the other part plowed. This method was to write them a letter of courtesy asking them if it would not be inconvenient or prejudicial to do me the favor of sending me the oxen and Negroes with which they were accustomed to plow and that I would send them an equal number of Negroes that they could employ in the same tasks and who would understand the Negro workers. That was the substance of the letter I sent to Messrs. Borel and Boutet having made the same proposition verbally to the other two and who gladly agreed to each send me a complete plow and I will reimburse them with what I promised to their satisfaction. The Acadians who came voluntarily from Vermilion I satisfied them with money for their day's wage and labor (as I have already explained to Your Lordship) after having consulted with Mr. Flamand as to the custom of the country so as not to overpay them and still keep them satisfied and content as they appeared to be. Besides the work of these and that of the planting came to plowing about thirty arpents.

Mr. Borel with whom I just finished talking to about this told me he has kept the letter I wrote him about the matter at the Atacapas and if Your Lordship wishes he will be pleased to send it to Your Lordship as soon as he arrives there.

The clause in the contract with these families in which Your Majesty obliges himself to assist and support them until the harvest of the first crop has made them not only look with sorrow upon this plot of ground but they also showed the greatest repugnance in accepting the part I assigned them and depending upon the advancement of the season in which they did not set foot the first two months and only went to care for it with some effort when they saw the abundant crop which the fertile soil promises and the firm resolution which I manifested to them that he who does not take care of his field will not have any help nor aid when the harvest is finished.

Regarding the question Your Lordship asked me about the hired Negroes who were employed in the establishment of New

Iberia. I should tell Your Lordship that since the beginning of April, the time in which, if my memory helps me, they began to work in the second establishment, the Negroes were constantly employed in transporting, about eight leagues from the first establishment the families and all their effects carrying the pieux which they had made there, and everything else that could be useful, in plowing and planting and taking care of seventy-five arpents of corn, twenty-five of rice, four or six of potatoes dividing them among the families; in planting and caring for the tobacco before it was distributed; in digging and caring for the plot of ground which contained the supply of corn and rice, in plowing in the same plot another piece of six arpents for the same end, in sowing and caring for about thirty-five arpents of corn which when the waters receded I had planted in the plowed ground of the first establishment. In making two large closed cabins, sixty feet long each one, one where some families were lodged, one house with a forge for the blacksmith; another for the two families of Artacho Prados, another for the food supply; two others for the Germans, another for the soldiers, another for Mr. Flamand, another for Mr. Henderson with a storehouse for the corn, another for the Ibañes family and a storehouse where the effects of the King are stored and at my house they have made a large cabin for making bricks, and a portion of this and another of shell which I made them put at the edge of the water of the first establishment intended for making lime, a big fence for keeping the oxen which are continually in use occupying themselves also in caring for these and other animals, in making necessary lumber for mounting the carpenter tools, carts for transporting the posts and other lumber, and big wagons for transporting the logs, in these and various other small jobs directed to this end the Negroes were employed until the end of August when I left there, having charged Mr. Henderson and Bervick to occupy the Negroes who remained there in storing materials and following the same system in helping the families in the work they could not do for themselves, charging Mr. Boutet to watch over everything with orders to Henderson and all the others to obey him.

This is what I can tell Your Lordship concerning the question which Your Lordship asked me. It seems important to me that

I should make it known to Your Lordship that it would be convenient that I leave as soon as possible with the Negroes I have appointed to go with me from the beginning up to now in order to conclude this year the placing of these families under the terms I have had the honor to place before Your Lordship or in those which Your Lordship will find more suitable.

May God, Our Lord, keep Your Lordship for many years. New Orleans, November 3, 1779.

I kiss Your Lordship's hand, your most attentive servant and obedient subject.

Francisco Bouligny (seal)

Senor Don Bernardo de Galbez.

Legajo no. 606

4.

My dear Sir,

I received Your Lordship's letter of March 7 in which you tell me to send you the account of expenses which the building of a *curial* church at this Post might entail. I inform Your Lordship that it is the small cost of fifty pesos for the materials and working men.

With this I send Your Lordship the report of the contracted families with specification of the boys and girls which each family has.

Equally the account of the utilities which remain with me, so that Your Lordship will dispose of them as you find convenient.

In regard to the live stock vaccine I did not send the note that each one has because the inhabitants are in the cultivation of the ground but at the first occasion I will send Your Lordship the note of each one, I have nothing more to communicate to Your Lordship. I pray Our Lord to guard your important life for many years. New Iberia, April 12, 1785.

I kiss Your Lordship's hand. Your most devoted and obligated servant.

Antonio Martinez (seal)

Senor Don Juan Morales.

Report naming the individuals who compose the new settlement of New Iberia in the year 1785.

Names of married men and number in family each have	Single young men	Single young ladies
Diego Romero	4	1
Bernardo Aponte	2	1
Francisco Ortiz	2	4
Contracted) Joseph de Poras single)		
Joseph Artacho	1	1
Gregorio Artacho		
Antonio Villatoro		
Juan Migues	2	
Francisco Balderas	1	
Juan Garido	2	
Gabril Lopez	1	
Juan Lopez	3	
Joseph Fernandez		1
Felis Lopez		
Francisco Segura		1
Gonzalo de Prados		2
Manuel de Prados		1
Julian de Agilar		
Rafael Vidal	2	1

Total number of families who live at this Post.

Married: 18. Their wives: 18; Single men: 1; Sons in families: 20; Daughters in families: 13.

New Iberia, April 12, 1785.   Antonio Martinez (seal)

Account of the implements which are at this Post of New Iberia which belong to the King.

Work axes	44
Demolishing ax	10
Useless ax	13
Hoes or spades	44
Bricklayer trowels	6
Gadanas	21
Ditto, used	8
Sickles	16
Files	114
Iron plows	5

Knives of the same 6
14 pairs of repaired hingles 14
Same 3 hinges without 3
Locks for doors 7
Saws *trauesal* 7
Same, used 1
Locks for doors, useless 11
Augers 13
Carpenter's iron brush 31
Chisels 10
Small useless saw blades 6
8 dozens links 8
Padlocks without keys 7
Whole iron bars 6
Pieces of iron bars 10
3 pieces of steel 3
2 useless hemp ropes.
New Iberia, Apsil 12, 1785.

                        Antonio Martinez (seal)[4]

[4]The Spanish documents were very difficult to translate due to fact that very little punctuation was used and because of the natural change in the language which has taken place in the past one hundred forty years. The spelling of many names was inconsistent, sometimes in the same document. It seems reasonable to believe, because of information in other records that in *Legajo no. 606*, in the list of the inhabitants in New Iberia in 1785, that the name "Diego Romero" should be "Miguel Romero."

SELECTED BIBLIOGRAPHY

A. Manuscripts

Archivo General de Indias, Seville, Spain.
   Papeles Procedentes de Cuba: Legajos 600, Legajos 606,
      Legajos 2358.
City of Jeanerette, City Hall, Jeanerette, Louisiana.
   City Minutes
City of New Iberia, City Hall, New Iberia, Louisiana.
   City Minutes
Iberia Parish Records, Courthouse, New Iberia, Louisiana.
   Original Conveyances
   Original Mortgages
   Police Jury Minutes
Louisiana Records, State Land Office, Baton Rouge, Louisiana.
   Tract Book, Southwest District.
Louisiana State Department Records, Baton Rouge, Louisiana.
St. Martin Church Records, St. Martinville, Louisiana.
St. Martin Parish Records, Courthouse, St. Martinville,
      Louisiana.
   Brand Book for the Attakapas District
   Marriage Index
   Miscellaneous Book
   Original Acts
   Sheriff Sale Book
   Succession Records
St. Peter's Church Records, New Iberia, Louisiana.
Town of Delcambre, City Hall, Delcambre, Louisiana.
   Town Minutes
United States Post Office Department Records, Washington, D. C.

B. Official Documents

A Compendium of the Ninth Census June 1, 1870, Washington,
      1872.
American State Papers, edited by Walter Lowrie et al. 38 vols.,
      Washington, 1833-1861.
County-Parish Boundaries in Louisiana. Prepared by the His-
      torical Records Survey Division of Professional and Serv-

ice Projects, Works Projects Administration, New Orleans, 1939.

Guide to Vital Statistics Records of Church Archives in Louisiana, I, Protestant and Jewish Churches, Louisiana State Board of Health, New Orleans, 1942.

Guide to Vital Statistics Records of Church Archives in Louisiana, II, Roman Catholic Churches, Louisiana State Board of Health, New Orleans, 1942.

Louisiana *Acts,* 1839, 14 Leg., 1 Sess., 1839.

Outline of the Physical Geography of the State of Louisiana, Compiled from published reports and manuscript notes by Eugene W. Hilgard, Department of the Interior, *Tenth Census of the United States,* Washington, 1880.

Report of the Productions of Agriculture as Returned at the Tenth Census (June 1, 1880), 22 vols., Washington, 1883.

Report of the Population of the United States at the Eleventh Census: 1890, 25 vols., Washington, 1895.

Report on the Statistics of Agriculture in the United States at the Eleventh Census: 1890, 25 vols., Washington, 1895.

Twelfth Census of the United States Taken in the Year 1900, 10 vols., Washington, 1902.

Walker, Francis A. *Ninth Census; The Statistics of the Wealth and Industry of the United States,* 3 vols., Washington, 1872.

C. Books, Pamphlets, and Articles

Arthur, Stanley Clisby, and George Kernion (ed.). *Old Families of Louisiana.* New Orleans, 1931.

Barde, Alexandre. *Histoire des Comites de Vigilance aux Attakapas.* Saint-Jean-Baptiste (Louisiane). Impr. du Meschacebe et de L'Avant-Coureur, 1861.

Chambers, Henry E. *A History of Louisiana.* 3 vols., Chicago and New York, 1925.

"The Church of the Attakapas 1750-1889," *American Catholic Quarterly Review,* XIV *(July, 1889),* pp. 462-487.

Coughey, John Walton. *Bernardo de Galvez in Louisiana 1775-1883.* Berkley, California, 1934.

Darby, William. *The Emigrant's Guide to the Western and Southwestern States and Territories Comprising a Geographical and Statistical Description of the States . . . Ac-*

companied by a Map of the United States . . . New York, 1818.

DeBow, J. D. B. (ed.). "Louisiana Historical Researches," *The Commercial Review of the South and West*, III (1847).

Duvallon, Berquin-(ed.). *Vue de la Colonie Espagnole du Mississippi . . . 1802 . . .* Paris, 1803.

Flint, Timothy. *A Condensed Geography and History of the Western States, or the Mississippi Valley*, 2 vols., Cincinnati, 1828.

—————. *Recollections of the Last Ten Years, Passed in Occasional Residences and Journeyings in the Valley of the Mississippi.* Boston, 1826.

Fortier, Alcee. *History of Louisiana*, 4 vols., New York, 1904.

—————. (ed.) *Louisiana; Comprising Sketches of Counties, Towns, Events, Institutions, and Persons Arranged in Cyclopedia Form*, 3 vols., Atlanta, 1914.

Gayarre, Charles. *History of Louisiana*, 4 vols., New Orleans, 1903.

Goodspeed Publishing Company. *Biographical and Historical Memoirs of Louisiana*, 2 vols., Chicago, 1892.

Iberia Parish Resources and Facilities. Survey by Iberia Parish Development Board, Published in Cooperation with State of Louisiana Department of Public Work Planning Division, Baton Rouge, 1942.

Jefferson, Joseph. *Autobiography.* New York, 1890.

Kane, Harnett T. *The Bayous of Louisiana.* New York, 1943.

Kinnaird, Lawrence (ed.). "Spain in the Mississippi Valley 1765-1794," II, III, IV, *Annual Report of the American Historical Asociation*, 1945, 4 vols., Washington, D. C. 1946.

Louisiana A Guide to the State. (Compiled by Workers of the Writers' Program of the W.P.A. in the State of Louisiana, American Guide Series), New York, 1945.

Louisiana Almanac and Fact Book, 1953-1954. New Orleans, 1953.

Louisiana Historical Quarterly, I-XXXIII (1917-1950), New Orleans.

A Louisiana Planter, "Prairies of Louisiana," *Niles' Weekly Register*, XIII (September, 1817), pp. 118-120.

Budda Temple in Jungle Gardens, Avery Island, Louisiana.

Horseradish seed pieces (from roots) and "Mulvaney" crowns in yards.

Moors, John Farwell. *History of the Fifty-second Massachusetts Volunteers.* Boston, 1893.

Notes for a History of St. Martin Parish. Made available through the courtesy of Honorable Edwin E. Willis, Congressman, Third Congressional District of Louisiana (1957).

Official Report Relative to the Conduct of Federal Troops in Western Louisiana. Compiled from Sworn Testimony Under Direction of Governor Henry W. Allen, Shreveport, April, 1865 (Reprint January, 1939).

Perrin, William Henry (ed.). *Southwest Louisiana Biographical and Historical.* New Orleans, 1891.

"Plantation Houses," *Louisiana Deep South,* Baton Rouge, (1954).

Raper, Arthur. "Farm Tenancy in the South," *Louisiana Schools* (January, 1940), pp. 5, 24.

Redwood, Allen C. "A Little World," *Scribner's Monthly,* XXII (August, 1881).

Richardson, F. D. "The Teche Country Fifty Years Ago," *The Southern Bivouac,* IV (1886), pp. 593-598.

Robin, C. C. *Voyages dans l'Interieur de la Louisiane . . . , 1802-1806.* 3 vols., Paris, 1807.

The South in the Building of the Nation. 13 vols., Richmond, c1909.

"Standard Market Data for New Iberia, Louisiana." Bulletin Published by the New Iberia *Daily Iberian,* n.d.

Survey of Federal Archives. Louisiana. *Ship Registers and Enrollments of New Orleans, Louisiana.* University, Louisiana, 1941. 6 vols.

Taylor, Richard. *Destruction and Reconstruction.* New York, 1879.

"Tour the Deep Southland," *Louisiana's Deep South,* Baton Rouge, (1954).

Warner, Chas. Dudley. "The Acadian Land," *Harper's Magazine,* LXXIV (February, 1887).

D. Unpublished Theses

Mestayer, Vivien A. "The History of the New Iberia High School, 1887 through 1950," M. A. Thesis, Louisiana State University, 1951.

Owen, James Kimbrough. "A Study in Local Government in

Louisiana," M. A. Thesis, Louisiana State University, 1940.

E. Newspapers

Baton Rouge *Morning Advocate,* November 25, 1951.

Breaux Bridge *The Attakapas Sentinel,* June 4, 1874.

Franklin *Planters' Banner,* September 20, 1845-July 22, 1847.

Lafayette *Daily Advertiser,* 1952, 1957.

New Iberia *Daily Iberian,* December 1893-June 1894, April 3-November 1, 1899, October 1, 1946-1961.

New Iberia *Democrat,* August 6, 1890-January 3, 1891.

New Iberia *Enterprise,* February 1885-July 1947.

New Iberia *Louisiana Sugar Bowl,* November 3, 1870-March 27, 1879.

New Iberia *Semi-Weekly Iberian,* June 16, 1900.

New Iberia, *Weekly Iberian,* July 1894-September 1946.

New Orleans *Catholic Action of the South,* June 25, 1953.

New Orleans *Catholic Action of the South,* June 25, 1953.

New Orleans *The Daily Picayune,* October 14, 1895.

New Orleans *The Times Democrat,* April 3, 1899.

New Orleans *The Times Picayune,* June 7, 1940, December 20, 1942.

Opelousas *Daily World,* November 3, 1955. (Supplement, St. Landry Parish 150th Anniversary Edition.)

St. Martin *Banner,* February 18, 1905.

INDEX

CPSIA information can be obtained at www.ICGtesting.com
Printed in the USA
LVOW08s2322290913

354595LV00001B/2/A